DATE			

◇ ◇ ◇

American Indian Science

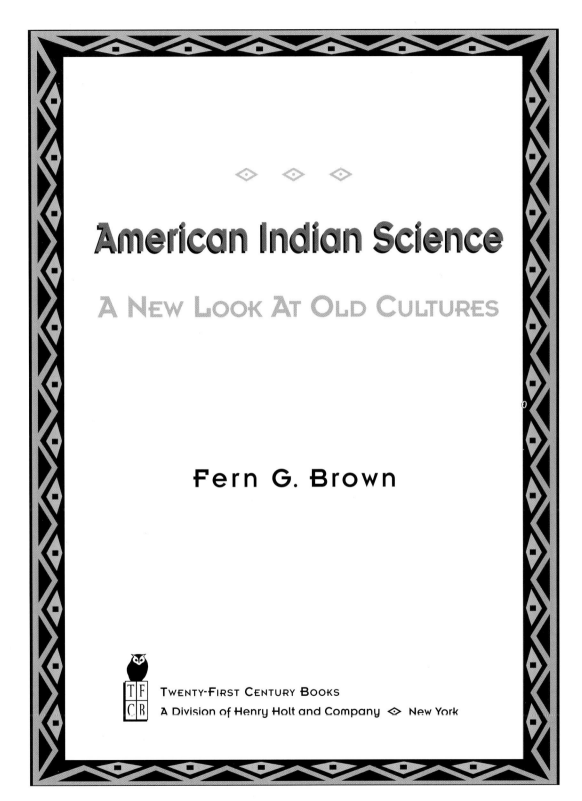

◇   ◇   ◇

American Indian Science

A NEW LOOK AT OLD CULTURES

Fern G. Brown

TWENTY-FIRST CENTURY BOOKS
A Division of Henry Holt and Company ◇ New York

Cover: An artist's re-creation of Cahokia, across the river from present-day St. Louis. Hundreds of years before Columbus, Cahokia was a leading commercial, religious, and political center.

Twenty-First Century Books
A Division of Henry Holt and Company, Inc.
115 West 18th Street
New York, NY 10011

Henry Holt® and colophon are trademarks of
Henry Holt and Company, Inc.
Publishers since 1866

Published in Canada by Fitzhenry & Whiteside Ltd.
195 Allstate Parkway, Markham, Ontario, L3R 4T8

Library of Congress Cataloging-in-Publication Data
Brown, Fern G.
American Indian Science: a new look at old cultures/Fern G. Brown.
p.   cm.
Includes bibliographical references and index.
Summary: Describes efforts to document the enormous contribution
made by early Native Americans to scientific knowledge.
1. Indians of North America—Science—Juvenile literature. 2. Civilization—Indian influences—
Juvenile literature. [1. Civilization—Indian influences. 2. Indians of North America.] I. Title
E98.S43B76   1997   96-48802
609.73'dc21   CIP
                                                                                                                  AC

ISBN 0-8050-3251-7
First Edition—1997
Designed by Kelly Soong

Printed in Mexico.
All first editions are printed on acid-free paper.∞

1 3 5 7 9 10 8 6 4 2

Photo credits
pp. 10, 13, 14: ©David W. Harp; p. 17: Arizona State Museum, University of Arizona, Helga Teiwes, photographer; p. 18 (top): ©G. Prance/Visuals Unlimited; p. 18 (bottom): ©Holt Studios International (Nigel Cattlin)/Photo Researchers, Inc.; p. 19: ©Charles Mann; p. 22: ©John Sohlden/Visuals Unlimited p. 23: R. Konig/Jacana/Photo Researchers, Inc.; pp. 24, 28: Transparency no. 5682(2) photo by Lynton Gardiner, Courtesy Dept. of Library Services, American Museum of Natural History; p. 27: Tod Legnick of FocusOne, the official photographer for Science Service Incorporated's 47th International Science and Engineering Fair; p. 33 (both): ©Illinois Historic Preservation Agency; p. 35: ©Mireille Vautier/Woodfin Camp; p. 38: ©Chuck O'Rear/Woodfin Camp; p. 41: ©Mark E. Gibson/The Stock-Market; p. 42: ©Malak; p. 45: Victor R. Boswell, Jr./ ©National Geographic Society Image Collection; p. 46: Thomas W. Melham, Jr./©National Geographic Society Image Collection; p. 48:©North Wind Pictures; pp. 50, 58: ©John D. Cunningham/Visuals Unlimited; p. 55: Neg. no. 323365, Courtesy Dept. of Library Services, American Museum of Natural History; pp. 56, 57: ©Denver Museum of Natural History Photo Archives; p. 59: Transparency no. 5591(2) photo by Lynton Gardiner, Courtesy Dept. of Library Services, American Museum of Natural History; p. 61: University of California, Lawrence Livermore National Laboratory; p. 62: ©Paula Lerner/Woodfin Camp.

CONTENTS

Introduction   7

One   **FARMING THE LAND**   11

Two   **MEDICINE AND HEALING**   21

Three   **ARCHITECTURE**   32

Four   **MATH AND ASTRONOMY**   44

Five   **TOOLS, WEAPONS, AND TECHNOLOGY**   54

Conclusion   65

For More Information   67

Glossary   72

Acknowledgments   74

Index   76

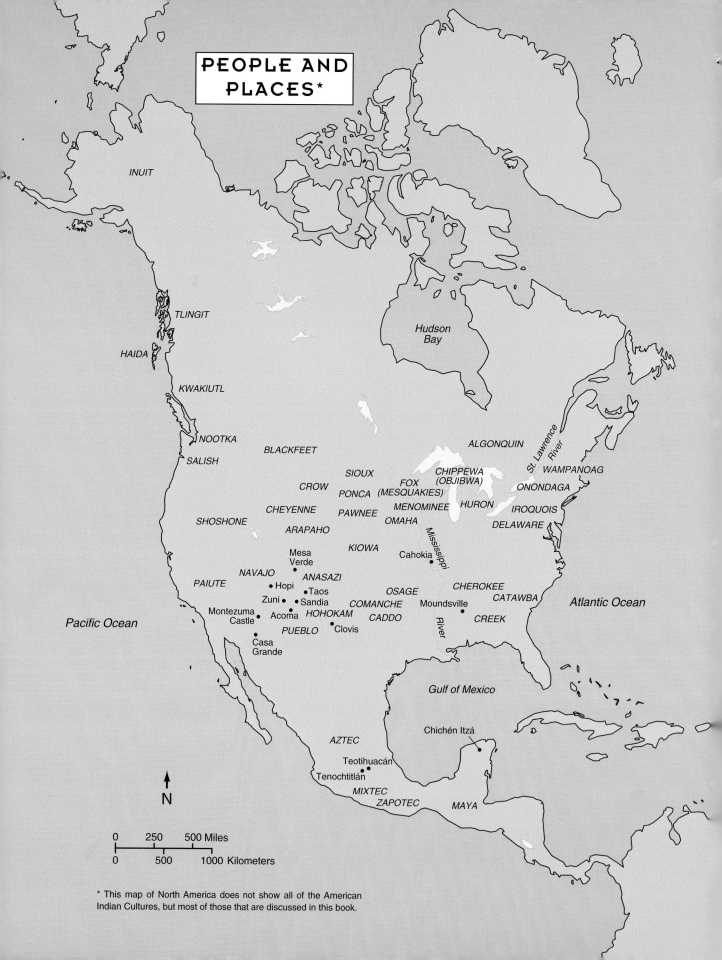

PEOPLE AND PLACES*

INUIT

TLINGIT

HAIDA

KWAKIUTL

NOOTKA

SALISH

BLACKFEET

Hudson Bay

ALGONQUIN

St. Lawrence River

SIOUX

CROW

PONCA

CHIPPEWA (OBJIBWA)

FOX (MESQUAKIES)

WAMPANOAG

ONONDAGA

CHEYENNE

PAWNEE

MENOMINEE

HURON

IROQUOIS

SHOSHONE

ARAPAHO

OMAHA

DELAWARE

KIOWA

Mesa Verde

NAVAJO

ANASAZI

• Hopi

Zuni • • Sandia
• Taos

Montezuma Castle •

Acoma

PAIUTE

OSAGE

Cahokia •

Mississippi

CHEROKEE

CATAWBA

Atlantic Ocean

COMANCHE

Moundsville •

CADDO

River

CREEK

HOHOKAM

PUEBLO

• Clovis

Pacific Ocean

Casa Grande

Gulf of Mexico

Chichén Itzá •

AZTEC

Teotihuacán •

N

Tenochtitlán •

MIXTEC

ZAPOTEC

MAYA

0   250   500 Miles

0   500   1000 Kilometers

* This map of North America does not show all of the American Indian Cultures, but most of those that are discussed in this book.

INTRODUCTION

The archaeological history of the native peoples of the Americas goes back more than thirty thousand years. By the time Columbus landed in what he called the "New World," it was anything but new. Civilizations had come and gone through the centuries. Large populations of peoples who spoke many different languages had already developed a diversity of thriving cultures and civilizations. They were all joined by a trade network that covered the entire northern continent.

◇ NATIVE AMERICAN ANCESTORS ◇

Who were the ancestors of today's Native Americans, and how did they come to be the earliest people living in North America? Archaeologists have found ancient Indian bones, weapons, tools, and art hidden in the earth. They have studied and dated their findings by various methods, mainly by measuring the amount of radioactivity in the carbon 14 (radiocarbon) found at the digs. After examining all the evidence they have pieced together a rather incomplete story.

Most scientists agree that at one time ice stretched from the North Pole as far south as what is now Wisconsin. It covered the eastern part of America, but some of the west was free from ice, especially in the valleys. Open land stretched along the plains country (Nebraska) up through the Mackenzie Valley in Canada and the Yukon in Alaska.

7

Other valleys in Siberia led into the heart of Asia. There was no Bering Strait to separate Siberia from Alaska; instead, a strip of land once formed a bridge that joined the two continents.

Scientists today believe that groups of prehistoric men and women came across the land bridge from Asia. For centuries they traveled on foot, roaming over the icy top of the world in small groups, tracking herds of wild animals. These hunters spoke different languages and had varied customs. As time passed they wandered down from the icy northland into the Great Plains and spread apart, some settling along the way. Others pushed on over high mountains and through dangerous jungles, heading south. They followed the sun to Florida and the islands of Tierra del Fuego lying off the extreme southern tip of South America.

Meanwhile the ice was slowly melting every year. North America became a country of rivers, lakes, and forests. Eventually, the level of the oceans rose, and the land bridge between Asia and North America was swallowed up. There are many theories, but enough has been discovered that most Euroamerican scientists believe these nomads from Asia are the ancestors of today's Indians.

Yet, others are as likely to say that the evidence is just as strong supporting the argument that some groups were always on this continent. They are believed to be the First People who were given Earth to live on by the Creator. Later, other groups migrated across the strait or came by sea.

One thing we do know for sure. The Indians settled and occupied homes, communities, and city-states throughout the Western Hemisphere. Where they lived—along the coast, in the woods, in the deserts, or on the prairies—influenced the way they lived. It affected their work, their dress, their language, and their crafts.

There were over 750 Native American tribes living in North American when the Europeans arrived. They had many names and spoke more than 350 languages. Besides farmers and hunters, there were astronomers, builders who constructed houses, engineers of irrigation systems, and health providers with a storehouse of medicinal knowledge.

◇ LOOKING BACK TO LOOK FORWARD ◇

Today, researchers are taking a fresh look at the cultures of America before Columbus. And with the advent of a new generation of Native Americans who are rediscovering the wisdom of their ancestors and reclaiming their heritage, there is a growing awareness of the enormous contribution made by early Native Americans to scientific knowledge. This reevaluation of the past stems in part from our attempts to find solutions to the environmental problems of modern civilization—polluted air, water, and land; our reliance on chemicals to grow foods and supplement our diets; the depletion of our natural resources; overcrowding and a technology out of control.

Much of what was once dismissed as superstition and myth by scientists trained in the scientific method is being reexamined. Whereas "Eurocentric Science" encompasses mostly the physical and mental sides of human beings, Indian science, or "indigenous science," encompasses all sides of a person, the spiritual and emotional as well as the mental and physical. It recognizes that all human beings are part of the earth and that every single thing in creation has a spirit and an equal right to exist. Although objects or forces may be unseen or inanimate, such as the wind, rocks, thunder, the tiniest pebble, or the highest mountain, they are related and they possess spirit.

In the words of Totanka Yotanka (Sitting Bull), religious leader and medicine man of the Hunkpapa Lakota, "In the morning when I walk barefoot on its soil I can hear the very heart of the holy earth."

This book focuses on the science of the American Indians—mainly those cultures of North America—and some of their achievements. We will discuss Native Americans' knowledge of agriculture and farming and their contribution to medicine and healing, math and astronomy, tools and technology, and architecture. Unfortunately, much knowledge has been lost, either through a systematic attempt to destroy native cultures or, perhaps more often, an ignorance of what was of value. As you read this book, bear in mind that we are looking at a great diversity of cultures that existed at different times over thousands of years.

Some of the roots of modern science are buried deep in historical sites across the Americas. These ancient roots still affect us today.

Strawberry popcorn, flour corn,
original southwest calico corn, and old-strain blue corn

ONE

Farming the Land

Imagine if the management of a modern-day supermarket decided to clear the shelves of all foods whose origins date back to early American Indian cultures. Great gaps would appear on the store's shelves and in the bins due to the removal of tomatoes, canned as well as fresh; corn, today America's basic crop; potatoes; all types of beans—lima, kidney, string, shell, pea; and much more. It has been said that America's greatest gift to the rest of the world was its great variety of foods.

◇ CORN ◇

Among the many foods developed by Indians, corn perhaps has made the greatest impact on the world. It was the staff of life for most Indians, much as wheat bread was for the Europeans. Today, the United States is the world's largest producer of corn. Besides using corn in many forms in our diets, it is the grain of choice for livestock feed. We are still finding new uses for corn, such as an ingredient in ethanol (for car fuel).

Corn was introduced from Peru and Mexico. Before the Europeans arrived, it was widely grown by native farmers, from the Northeast to the South, from Canada all the way to the hot, dry deserts of the southwest United States. It was cooked in many ways: roasted, boiled, parched and pounded into meal, or made into corn soup, dumplings, hominy, or succotash (corn and lima beans). Hominy, a dish made from corn husks, was eaten plain, dried, or ground into grits. Many people are surprised to learn that southern grits is an Indian dish.

When planting corn, many Indians, among them the Pemaquid and Wampanoag of the Northeast, used a system called hilling, which centered on a milpa (a small field). Rows of small hills about two feet apart were readied, and corn kernels were planted in each hill. The hilling method was an idea European settler-farmers borrowed from the Indians, and it was used from Colonial times until the 1930s.

European settlers also adopted the Indian custom of planting seed rather than sowing it. Old World grains had small seeds that the farmer threw out by the handful. Because Indian corn seeds were larger, farmers were able to select the kernels to be planted in each hill. This practice led to the development of hundreds of plant varieties, such as sweet corn, popcorn, and flint corn.

PRACTICING GENETICS

Through generations of trial and error, Native Americans seemed to understand genetics. Because they wanted to grow better corn, farmers began to fertilize each plant by putting corn pollen on its silk. Gradually, they went further and took the pollen from one kind of corn and fertilized the silk of another variety. This process resulted in corn with the combined characteristics of the two parent stalks. We call this process hybridization.

To protect the kernels from pests and weather, some Indian farmers bred corn to have a husk around it. The husk did its job—probably too good a job. Corn can't reproduce unless the farmer removes the husk. That's why it never grows wild.

COMPANION PLANTING

The Iroquois, among others, called corn, beans, and squash the "three sisters" and planted them together. The delicate bean plants were shaded from the hot sun by the broad leaves of the corn plant, and the corn stalk provided a pole for the bean and squash vines to climb.

Squash vines also sprawled on the ground between the corn and bean plants, making an excellent ground cover and keeping out unwanted plants. These vines caught and held the rain, preventing soil erosion from wind or water. Because beans are a good source of nitrogen in the soil, they helped the corn and squash grow. This method of growing corn, beans, and squash together is still used today on many Maya farms in the Yucatan.

Recently, researchers looking closely at this ancient farming practice have found that

July in a "three-sisters" garden: The squash plant begins to send out its large umbrellalike leaves, which will soon cover the ground; the beans are beginning to climb the corn stalk, and the corn has not yet tasseled.

the combination of corn, beans, and squash helps reduce destruction of the plants by pests. That's because these plants attract the insects that prey on the pests, and corn loss is kept to a minimum without the use of insecticides.

◇ POTATOES ◇

The first white (Irish) potatoes were cultivated by Indians of the Andes. Later, they became a major part of the Navajo diet. When the Spaniards introduced potatoes into

◇   ◇   ◇

LEARNING FROM THE PAST

Dr. Jane Mt. Pleasant, of Iroquois descent, is an agronomist at Cornell University in upstate New York. She is carrying out an experimental program to find better ways to raise crops without overuse of pesticides and soil depletion. Much of her research centers on the "three sisters"—corn, beans, and squash.

According to University of Vermont agronomist Frederick Magdoff, Mt. Pleasant is "one of the younger generation of scientists . . . who are looking at all sorts of alternative agricultural practices, some new, but some going back thousands of years."

Europe, people there were not a bit excited about them. Yet it wasn't long before they realized that a field of potatoes produced more nutritious food in a shorter time than the same field planted with a grain. Potatoes were easy to grow in all kinds of soil; they did not need to be milled or processed, and they could be stored for nearly a year without spoiling. People made soups, pancakes, bread, dumplings, and pies out of potatoes, and they became a staple crop of many European countries, especially Ireland. Maybe one day scientists will enlarge the range of the potato to feed the people in places like Bangladesh as it now feeds those of Europe.

◇ COTTON ◇

Although the farmers didn't need machinery to process pototoes, another crop, cotton, kept the looms busy. The long-strand cotton of the American Indians was of much better quality than the cotton of the Old World. For thousands of years before the Europeans came to America, the Indians had been using this carefully developed cotton to weave some of the world's finest textiles. Many pieces of these early cloths can be seen in museums today with their colors and designs still intact.

◇ TOBACCO ◇

Tobacco was another Indian crop that helped the European settlers that grew it to prosper. Colonists experimented with the Indian methods of growing and cultivating to find a good tobacco that could be mass produced and shipped. The product was a combination of both technologies. Tobacco cultivation spread throughout the South and with it developed the slavery-based plantation system.

◇ IRRIGATION ◇

For more than two thousand years before the first Europeans came to America, the Hohokam were farming in the southern Arizona desert around present-day Phoenix. There was very little rainfall, so they dug canals—by hand—that directed the flow of water from the Salt and Gila rivers to their dry fields. A canal might be 8 to 14 miles (13 to 22 kilometers) long and about 6 feet (1.8 meters) deep. But some were as deep as 15 feet (4.5 meters) and 90 feet (27 meters) wide. Smaller ditches formed a network over the fields and connected with the main canal so that water, when needed, could be sent to all

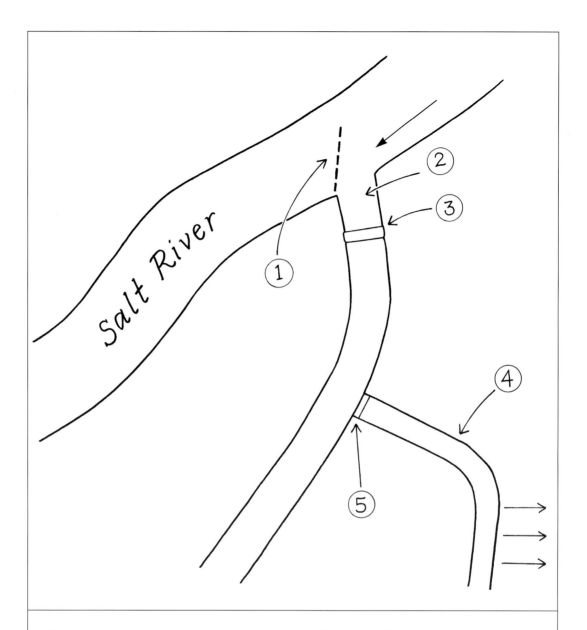

Hohokam engineers used the waters of the Salt and Gila rivers to irrigate their land. Archaeologists speculate that they built a *weir*, a dam, (1) into the river at the entrance to a main canal (2) to divert the water from the river. Here a headgate (3) was constructed to control the flow of water. From the main canal, distribution canals (4) carried the water to smaller branches and onto the fields. A diversion gate (5) controlled the flow of water into the distribution canal.

sections of the field. This way of watering the fields was one of the most advanced systems ever built by a preindustrial society. The debt owed the ancient Hohokam is evident in Phoenix today where some of their old canals are still in use.

The Paiute used temporary ditches to irrigate their land. In the spring when the snow began to melt, they built dams of boulders and brush across the beds of mountain streams to divert the water to their fields. Pueblo Indians built ditches along the mountain slopes to carry water to their crops.

One of the most advanced agricultural systems was the Mexican chinampas, or floating gardens. These were man-made islands 30 feet (9 meters) by 330 feet (100 meters) wide, formed by digging canals to drain swamps. Crops were easily watered by scooping out water from the canals.

The large Hohokam irrigation systems were in operation from A.D. 600 to 1450. Hundreds of miles of abandoned canals have now been documented by archaeologists in the Salt River Valley. According to anthropologist Jerrry Howard of the Mesa Southwest Museum in Phoenix, the Hohokam appeared to have covered over 110,000 acres (44,517 hectares) with the irrigation networks.

ANCIENT NATIVE CROPS INTEREST SCIENTISTS TODAY

According to Mark Dafforn of the National Academy of Science in Washington, D.C., scientific studies were conducted between 1982 and 1991 on amaranth. "Amaranth is rich in lysine [an important amino acid]," he said. "Its young green leaves contain calcium, iron, and phosphorus. They taste somewhat like spinach or artichoke, and the seeds are high in protein. This native grain shows great promise for feeding the world."

Amaranth (top right) may be popped or toasted and used in breads and salad dressings. One can also purchase amaranth flour, amaranth cornbread mix, and amaranth pancake mix.

Agricultural scientists at the Rodale Research Center at Kutztown, Pennsylvania, have provided amaranth seeds and technical help to researchers in Peru, Mexico, China, and other countries. They are confident that the plant can fight malnutrition in dry places.

Another ancient cereal crop that interests scientists is quinoa (lower right), a frost and drought-resistant grain grown in the high Andes. The Inca used it as an ingredient in soup. When boiled, the grain appears translucent. It is a fast-cooking, nutritious low-fat source of dietary fiber and protein. Because it is believed that eating more fiber and less fat is good nutrition, families today are adding quinoa to their soups, stews, casseroles, salads, and cooked cereals. Quinoa is now grown successfully in Colorado and New Mexico and is sold in supermarkets and health food stores.

◇ ◇ ◇

PRESERVING CROP DIVERSITY

At the Native Seeds/SEARCH, a nonprofit seed conservation organization headquartered at the Tucson Botanical Gardens, they are working to conserve native crops passed on to us by the indigenous peoples of the Southwest. Their projects include demonstration gardens, promotion of traditional foods to control diabetes, distribution of seeds to farmers and gardeners, a major regional seedbank, and the sponsorship of the Traditional Native American Farmers Association. The 1997 catalog for seed listings contains more than three hundred varieties of native crops for gardens.

◇ INDIANS AS TEACHERS ◇

When Harve Gallup, of Pontiac, Illinois, was asked if as a modern farmer he has been influenced by Native American agriculture, he said, "Yes. Around Illinois we live by an old Indian rule, 'Take care of the soil and it will take care of you.' "

Since European contact in 1492, to the present day, Native American farmers have taught others how to care for the soil and grow and process new plants. Today, the world is eating only a small amount of species (fewer than twenty-five), and we could run out of food. We need to grow more high-yield, nutritious grains. That's why scientists are experimenting with ancient native Aztec and southwest Indian grains, such as amaranth and quinoa (KEEN-wa), hoping to get a higher, more nutritious yield.

Indians have made valuable contributions to our society in the field of agriculture. They have discovered or domesticated more than half the modern world's major food crops. Whether teaching New World methods of farming and irrigation to the Europeans in the past or helping to restore ancient foods to the modern world's diet, Native Americans have never wavered from maintaining their intimate relationship with the land.

T W O

Medicine and Healing

Long before the earliest contact with European explorers there was Indian medicine, rich with symbolism and beauty. Although medicine and religion in our society are two separate functions, Indian healing combined medicine and religion. Medicine men were as highly respected as the bravest leaders in battle. Pharmacist, doctor, surgeon, all at the same time, these skilled healers treated disease, performed operations, and worked cures among their tribes. They used a blend of ritual, religion, and native healing herbs and plants to keep their people healthy.

◇ OUR DEBT TO INDIAN MEDICINE ◇

For a long time, European doctors thought that Native Americans had no real medical knowledge. Yet Indian medicine was at least on a par and in some ways ahead of the medical knowledge at that time, which had not advanced far from medieval days.

While Indians were using poultices and herbs to cure, European physicians still attached living leeches to patients to "suck out" the bad blood. Muslim doctors burned their patients with hot charcoal to heal them, and physicians in the Orient prescribed potions of dragon bones mixed with flavorings to make people well.

Centuries later, Western scientists began to take a good look at Indian healing practices. Some were found to be worthless, but a great many Indian treatments and drugs turned out to be valuable. It was then that modern scientists began to realize their debt to Native Americans. Dr. Frederick Banting, the discoverer of insulin, credited Indian healers with laying the groundwork for his important discovery.

Aspirin, one of the world's most widely used drugs, is based on compounds Indian healers long ago extracted from the leaves and bark of the willow tree to cure headaches and minor pains.

A colorless, gelatinous material known as petroleum jelly is another medicine gift from the Indians. Native healers were the first to use today's popular skin ointment to protect wounds and to promote healing.

Practices such as massage, hypnosis, visualization, and diet were often part of the treatment of mind and body by Indian healers. These therapies, including ways to manage stress, have been rediscovered and today are being called "alternative medicine" by various health providers.

We can also thank Native Americans for drugs that have been officially listed in *The Pharmacopeia of the United States of America*—more than 170 healing plants and herbs. Among them are cascara sagrada, lobelia, puccoon, cohosh, and dockmackie.

◇　　◇　　◇

THE BUCKTHORN'S BARK

Cascara sagrada is the most widely used cathartic in the world. It is still used in the U.S. *Pharmacopeia* because no synthetic substitute has been found to take its place. Cascara sagrada is made from the bark of the buckthorn tree (*Rhamnus purshiana*) and was given the name of "sacred bark" by Europeans who were impressed by its mildness and efficiency.

◇ THE SHAMAN, OR MEDICINE MAN ◇

Basic Indian treatment of wounds or other injuries where the cause was known usually worked well. Treatment of fractures and sprains or snake and insect bites also had good results. But if a person had a disease where the cause was unknown and ordinary medicines didn't bring a cure, then Indians turned to shamanistic practices such as prayers, dances, charms, beating drums, or shaking rattles.

Medicine men (shamans) were respected and feared in their villages. It was believed that they received their supernatural powers from the Creator. In some tribes medicine men were also chiefs, as were Totanka Yotanka (Sitting Bull) and Geronimo.

◇ PEYOTE ◇

Peyote is a thornless cactus that grows naturally from central Mexico to southern Texas. It is often found in clusters in the shade of taller plants.

If the healer had done his best to treat an illness and the patient was still ill, then the medicine man would visit the spirits. For example, in Mexico, to put themselves in a spiritual state, the Huichol Indian healers ate or brewed peyote tea, made from a wild cactus.

Peyote contains several alkaloids, the most powerful of which is mescaline. When people take it, peyote creates hallucinations. Called a sacred substance by Aztec priests, peyote continued to be used by Indians in northern Mexico over the next three centuries. By the time of the American Civil War, the use of peyote as a part of a religious ceremony (similar to the use of a wafer in the Christian religion) had spread to the southwestern part of the United States, reaching the Caddo Indians of Texas. Then, it spread north to the Comanche and Kiowas and on to the Cheyenne,

Osage, Arapaho, and other Great Plains Indians. In the twentieth century, peyote was adopted by Indians living around the Great Lakes and the Canadian border. Christian missionaries and others tried unsuccessfully to prevent the use of peyote in traditional native religions. Peyote was mainly used in Indian rituals, but it was also used for healing purposes by both Indians and whites.

In 1918, the Native American Church was incorporated. One of the beliefs of the church is that as Christ came to the whites, peyote came to the Indians. In this church, when peyote is taken as a sacrament, it is done in worship, with songs and prayers for the sick. It is thought to be too sacred to be abused by recreational use.

Peyote was used by South Texas Mexicans as a drink to reduce fever and as a lotion for feet and head. Tribes of southern Arizona chewed the root and made a poultice from it to put on fractures, large open wounds, and snakebites. Among the Kansas Potawatomis it helped rheumatism and paralysis. For some tribes in Oklahoma, it also proved to be a valuable remedy for certain problems of the nervous system. And Indians as well as U.S. Army surgeons used peyote as a painkiller.

◇ THE HEALING PROCESS ◇

Medicine men from tribe to tribe used different methods to heal their patients. However, some processes were used universally. Drums or rattles are a prime example because most healers had great confidence in the power of the music of these instruments.

Certain ritual objects such as the medicine bag or bundle were an important part of the ceremony. Usually handed down from father to son or given to a new medicine man by his teacher, these objects were very valuable. Some medicine bags were made of animal skin and contained charms and fetishes, such as deer tails and medicine sticks, which could be used as an offering, a warning, or an invitation. Sometimes, a medicine bag contained roots and herbs,

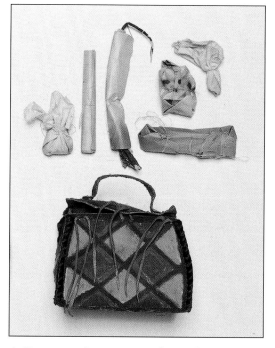

A Sioux medicine man's bag of traditional herbal remedies

paints, and other objects. One Menominee chief had sixty articles in his bundle, and it was known as a "sixty song bag."

As stated in Virgil J. Vogel's *American Indian Medicine*, in modern times, from the religious viewpoint (which was always uppermost to the Indian), the medicine bundle was perhaps the most important ritual object.

Many tribes, such as the Onondagas, conducted ceremonies to bless their herbs and make them powerful. Most Indians believed that herbs and plants that tasted bad were more beneficial because the demons in the body that had caused the disease would taste them, too, and leave the body.

◇ INDIAN HEALTH ◇

In many Indian cultures life was hard and the people were not disease free, but early Europeans observed that American Indians were relatively healthy and had very little deformity. They were comparing the standard of health in Europe with that of the Indians. When the Europeans came, however, they brought with them contagious diseases from their urban centers such as scarlet fever, smallpox, measles, and typhoid. Because the natives lacked immunity, these diseases often became epidemics and sometimes wiped out entire villages.

Although diseases varied in different regions, many of the other illnesses that Indians had came from living outdoors. Especially in the cold areas they were prone to diseases such as arthritis, pneumonia, dysentery, and other digestive disorders. But diseases such as cancer, heart disease, and neurological disturbances were rare.

◇ INDIAN MEDICAL PRACTICES ◇

An experienced medicine man usually knew many plants, herbs, and trees that he could use in his cures. Sometimes, bark and leaves of a tree were boiled and made into a strong tea, or herbs were chewed or pounded into a fine powder. After these medicines were mixed with a little water to form a paste, they were taken orally or put on a wound.

Some medicine men dried the leaves of jimsonweed plants, and patients smoked them in a pipe to treat diseases such as asthma and epilepsy. The plant was also used to soothe people. Today, the chemicals in the flower are distilled and used as a tranquilizer.

One of the most common ailments that plagued people in North America was snakebite. White settlers, to whom this was a new problem, assumed that the Indians had the correct remedies because snakebite happened so often. Suction at the site of the bite was used by most Indian healers. Then some form of plant or herb was applied. Many different plants were said to cure snakebite, such as the Fern root and Seneca snakeroot used by the southern Indians.

When a Creek was bitten by a snake, he immediately chewed some of the root he carried in a pouch. Then, he applied the quid to the wound. This ritual was repeated as long as was necessary, according to the severity of the bite. Metaphorically, the poison and the antidote fought each other until the poison was expelled through the same path it had entered and the patient was cured.

If the offending snake was caught, it would be cut up and pieces of muscle, rattle, or entrails were applied to the wound. This ritual was done with the thought in mind that the antidote for the bite was in the fat of the snake's flesh. If the snake was not captured, other greasy substances were prescribed to effect the cure.

The Delaware Indians used a plant called lion's-heart (*Prenanthes rubicunda*) to combat snakebite. The juice of the plant was boiled in milk and drunk, while the steeped leaves were applied to the wound. This method was also used in Virginia.

Besides these and many more plants, dozens of herbs were also used as Indian remedies for snakebite.

Some southwestern cultures practiced the Snake Dance, where participants were bitten by adult rattlesnakes but did not become ill. Because they had previously been bitten by young snakes with weak venom, and later by snakes of gradually increased ages, the dancers could withstand the bite of the adult.

The juice from the stems and leaves of jewelweed helped cure poison ivy, and the boiled leaves of horsemint were used to cure acne. There were also several remedies for nosebleeds, stomachaches, and bowel problems.

◇ INDIAN KNOWLEDGE OF DRUGS ◇

When trade ships from Europe brought malaria to America, an Indian drug made from cinchona, or Peruvian bark (many species), was found to help patients with the disease. It produced quinine, an active ingredient in chloroquine. The introduction of quinine was the beginning of modern pharmacology—knowledge of drugs. Before the discovery of quinine, malaria killed about two million people a year throughout the world. Until derivatives and synthetics became popular, quinine was the chief antimalarial drug.

The cure for scurvy is another example of indigenous knowledge of pharmacology. In November 1535, the French explorer Jacques Cartier and his men could not leave

CONSERVING A VALUABLE RESOURCE

College student Kendra Bird is an International Science Fair scholarship winner for her research on taxol, a drug derived from the inner bark of the Western yew (*Taxus brevifolia*) and used to treat ovarian and breast cancer. Because four yew trees must be killed to extract one gram of taxol, Bird's research centers on finding a natural replacement for this important anticancer agent.

Bird is a Blackfoot Indian from Browning, Montana, where the Western yew once grew abundantly.

Canada because their ships were frozen in the St. Lawrence River near the Huron settlement of Hochelaga, site of present-day Montreal. After a few months, several sailors began to feel sick, and one by one they died. When Cartier saw that the Hurons who had the same disease had been cured while his men were dying, he asked the natives for help. The Huron women showed him how to make a tonic from the bark and needles of an evergreen tree they called "annedda" (probably hemlock or pine). It contained a large amount of vitamin C, the cure for scurvy, and every sailor that was treated with it got well in a week.

No one had ever heard of vitamin C, but through centuries of trial and error, Indians had come upon a remedy for scurvy. Europeans thought scurvy was caused by bad air.

More than two hundred years after Cartier's experience with scurvy, Dr. James Lind, a naval surgeon, having heard of the incident, began experiments that proved scurvy was caused by lack of vitamin C in the diet.

◇ THE SWEAT LODGE ◇

Probably the most universal item used for illness and cleanliness was the sweat lodge. A sweat lodge could be an earth mound or a bundle of bent saplings covered by hides, grass, or blankets. It could also be an underground structure that was entered by a tunnel. The steam was produced by heating stones, placing them in an enclosed space, and drenching them with water. Many modern health clubs, borrowing the idea from the Indians, offer steam baths to their members.

◇ TREATING WOUNDS, FRACTURES, AND DISLOCATIONS ◇

Successful cures or treatments of wounds, fractures, and dislocations by Indian healers had been reported by white medical doctors who had observed their practices. Indians used many types of dressings, washes, and powders to help wounds drain. Perhaps President James Garfield might not have died of an infection from a bullet wound if his physicians had known about the Indian method of dressing wounds and keeping them clean.

The Sioux and Shoshone healers had a good knowledge of human anatomy and were able to set broken bones. After setting a bone, the medicine man wrapped it in a piece of rawhide (untanned animal skin) that had been soaked in water until it was soft. He then tied it in place with rawhide strips. As the hide dried, it molded to the arm or leg, forming a cast.

◇ GASTROINTESTINAL DISTURBANCES ◇

To relieve abdominal pain, no matter what the cause, Indians used massage, hot stones, moxas (hot poultices of ashes mixed with water), and the fleece of rabbit's or bird's down as binders to hold the poultice together.

Before applying massage, the Cherokee Indian healer warmed his hands over live coals, then rubbed the patient's sore place in a circle with his right hand, taking care to apply most of the pressure with his palm.

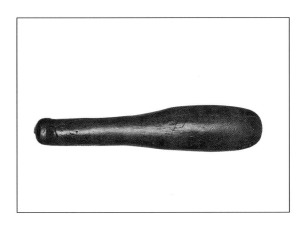

Some Indian healers used a stomach pusher to ease a patient's abdominal pain.

28

◇ DISEASES OF THE RESPIRATORY TRACT ◇

The common cold, bronchitis, and lung infections (with a few exceptions) were all treated alike. Medicine men made inhalers by putting certain plants, herbs, or roots on hot coals, and the patient was told to breathe the fumes. Then a tent was made from a blanket and placed around the fire and over the patient's head. Some of us do the same today when we have laryngitis. With a towel over our heads, we breathe fumes of medicated hot water.

Many different plants and herbs were used to cure a cold. For example, the Dakotas, Pawnees, Poncas, and Omahas burned the twigs of the red cedar (*Thuja plicata*), while both the patient and the fumigant were enclosed in a blanket. To a Comanche, juniper leaves were the best remedy for getting rid of a cold. The Catawbas preferred to boil a wild herb called pennyroyal (*Hedeoma pulegioides*) and drink it to rid themselves of the sneezes.

California Indians used a gum plant called *Grindelia robusta* to cure their bronchial troubles. The Utes also gave the plant to patients to cure coughs. After drying the entire wild bergamot plant (*Monarda fistulosa*), the Flambeau Ojibwas boiled it to get the oil. It was inhaled for catarrh (inflammation of mucous membranes, especially those of the nose and throat) and bronchial infections. The Menominees used the leaves and flowers of the same plant either alone or with other herbs and brewed a tea as a remedy for catarrh.

To cure lung trouble, the Mesquakies used both the black and white oak. They mixed the inner bark of the black oak with other roots for a remedy. Mesquakies also drank a tea made from boiling the inner bark of the white oak, to expel phlegm from the lungs. Yerba santa, an evergreen shrub, also called holy herb or mountain balm, was a great medicine among the Indians of southern Utah, Arizona, and California. For lung problems the dry leaves were chewed or smoked, or a tea made from them was drunk. Most Indian medicines were stored in skins to keep them clean and dry.

◇ SURGERY AND ANATOMY ◇

How did Indian surgeons compare with European doctors? Several reports by white doctors said that the Indians' technique for amputating a human limb was excellent, since operations depended on getting the job done quickly. Joints were amputated by a flint knife. To stop bleeding, the Indian surgeon then sealed the blood vessels with stones heated red hot. Deer tendons, human hair, vegetable fibers, and fibers of the soft, durable basswood were used to close the wound or cut. If the patient bled a lot, spider webs or pulverized puffball mushrooms helped stop the bleeding.

The Indian surgeon also knew a great deal about medicines for pain to put the patient "under." When it came to anesthetics, many Indian cultures were hundreds of years ahead of the Europeans.

◇ EVALUATING INDIAN MEDICINE ◇

Western scientists comparing the practice of medicine among the Indians with other medical practices of the day found there wasn't much difference. Sometimes, the Indians were ahead of other civilizations at the same stage of development. The medicine man's bag contained some excellent remedies based on sound procedures.

Many species of plants and herbs the Indians gathered for medicines are beginning to disappear, along with the knowledge of how to use them. Although Indians who live on reservations are more likely to preserve some of the old traditions, the younger generation is leaning toward Western medicine. As Mark J. Plotkin said in *Tales of a Shaman's Apprentice*, "Every time an old shaman dies, it's as if a library has burned to the ground."

Those who recognize the value of the thousands of years of native knowledge want to preserve it, so they are asking Indian healers to pass on the knowledge, which they are doing.

Recently, a company called Shaman Pharmaceuticals was formed in San Francisco, California, to discover and develop therapies to combat major human diseases. An ethnobotanist-physician team works with a native healer to identify the plants that heal-

◇ ◇ ◇

FIGHTING A TWENTIETH-CENTURY DISEASE

For the past three years, Native Seeds/SEARCH (NS/S) has offered information about the benefits of some plant foods that help prevent and control adult-onset diabetes. Diabetes is now a major health problem among Native Americans. Many traditional Native American foods, such as beans, chia, psyllium seed, and cholla buds have proven to be effective in regulating blood sugar. These foods keep sugar from being released into the blood and can be incorporated into a low-fat, high-fiber diet. In 1993, some members of the Tohono O'odham Nation working with the NS/S staff took part in a diabetes research project that gained worldwide attention.

ers have used to treat specific diseases. Traditional healers have seen the therapeutic effects of these local plants on humans for generations, and their knowledge and methods of preparation for healing save time, energy, and money in the drug discovery process.

The active compounds from these plants are chemically separated. Then the pure compounds are isolated and tested in university and botanic garden laboratories for activity against the disease. A board of scientific advisers helps decide which trees or plants to harvest and investigate further to develop into medicine.

Compounds are in technical trials now for herpes simplex virus and traveler's diarrhea. In addition, Shaman is doing preclinical testing on a number of other compounds that show potential for the treatment of Type 2 diabetes.

In 1989, Shaman Pharmaceuticals founded the Healing Forest Conservancy. This nonprofit organization returns a percentage of its profits from these potential medicines to the natives who taught us about the plants and to the countries where these plants grow. By promoting conservation of tropical forests, the conservancy is sustaining plant life—particularly medicinal plants—and thus sustaining tradition and saving the culture.

Other major drug companies are also looking for cures for AIDS, cancer, and Alzheimer's disease. Working with Native Americans, they, too, are examining and testing Indian healing plants to develop powerful new medicines.

Thus, medicine today is a joint effort enriched by contributions from both the Indian healers and modern technology.

T H R E E

Architecture

When we speak of the role that architecture played in Native American life, we are not just talking about the various types of homes and villages they built. We are also considering their use of the space around them in relation to their religious beliefs, social customs, and environment.

The Indians not only adapted to the climates where they had settled and used the natural materials they found there to build, but also took into account the function of the buildings. Anthropologist Peter Nabokov and coauthor California architect Robert Easton wrote in *Native American Architecture*, "Their traditions were their blueprints; social rules their building code."

Native Americans developed the engineering skill to build many types of structures, from impressive earthen mounds to cities on high cliffs. Indian communities were of various sizes. The little Paiute villages had barely one hundred residents, but there were also large Mayan cities such as Tikal and Copan. The city of Teotihuacán in the central valley of Mexico had a population of two hundred thousand at its height.

◇ MOUNDS ◇

Thousands of Indian mounds and earthworks have been found scattered throughout the central and eastern United States. Probably constructed by various tribes over a long period, mounds provide fascinating evidence of American Indians and their early technology. Mounds come in all shapes and sizes, large and small, oval, square or round. Some are shaped to resemble a snake, a bird, or an animal such as a buffalo, deer, or cougar.

Besides being the sites of homes and temples, mounds had many other uses. Many were built as fortifications, others served as foundations for various structures, and some were burial places. Objects found in and near the mounds tell the story of the people who used them.

Many mound cities arose, such as the one at Etowah, in northwestern Georgia; Spiro, in Oklahoma; Moundville in northwestern Alabama; and at Cahokia, in Illinois.

There are 120 mounds in Cahokia, the largest being Monks Mound. It rises in terraces and towers 100 feet (30 meters) above the Mississippi River, covering nearly 15 acres (6 hectares). The city once had a population of thirty thousand people, who lived in huge complexes.

An aerial view of Monks Mound, the largest prehistoric earthen mound in North America and one of sixty-eight mounds to be seen today at Cahokia, near Collinsville, Illinois.

Cahokia was inhabited from about A.D. 700 to 1400 and covered nearly 6 square miles (15.5 square kilometers). Its broad central plaza was used for ceremonies, sporting events, and business.

The center at Moundville, Alabama, grew into one of the largest and most important religious, political, and economic centers of western Alabama. Most of its people lived in outlying villages or on small farms and came to town on special occasions. The chief and his extended family lived above the plaza in homes on mounds. A temple mound stood in the center where ceremonies and rituals were conducted. At the height of its importance, Moundville covered 370 acres (150 hectares) and included twenty mounds, the largest of which was 60 feet (18 meters) high and covered an acre and a quarter (.6 hectare).

◈ TYPES OF STRUCTURES AND MATERIALS ◈

Wherever Indians lived, they built homes that were suited to the climate. Although their choice of building materials was limited to the materials they found on their land, such as wood, bark, stone, earth, snow, grass, skins, and leaves, they managed to make the most of them.

Indian buildings were always constructed according to tradition. The builder needed special skills and tools that were usually handed down from the old to the young at specific times.

EARTH LODGES

The Pawnee of the central plains are one of the tribes that built earth-covered houses called earth lodges. To enter the circular lodges, one had to go through a long, tunnel-like passageway. The floors were dug out to about 2 or 3 feet (.6 to .9 meters) to leave a unique earthen bench all the way around the inside of the house. When raising a lodge, the Pawnee began with four center support posts and placed beams across them. Then they packed layers of willow branches, sod, and mud tightly around this frame and over the top to form a domed roof with a smoke hole. There were no windows and the single entrance always faced east, where the sun rises.

THE HOGAN

In the Navajo language the word *hogan* means "home place." The earth with which hogans were covered helped keep them warm in the winter and cool in the summer. Inside, they were mostly circular, single rooms, heated by a central fireplace or wood-burning stove, with a hole in the roof or a stovepipe to release smoke. Like the Pawnee's earth lodge door, a hogan's door always faced east, to honor the sun.

Because religion was an important part of Navajo day-to-day life, the origin of the

Navajo hogan was also bound up in their religion. The great Talking God, the maternal grandfather of all the other gods or spirits, is said to have created the first hogan—a male hogan. Talking God also gave the Navajos a second, or female, hogan with a domed roof. Hogans are considered to be alive and must be periodically purified and fed. This is done with special songs and other rites. The floor areas are divided into male (south) and female (north). A house was usually abandoned when an occupant died.

To erect a modern hogan, the builder must get tribal council approval. At a Navajo reservation today, one would probably see all types of homes. A new, modern hogan might stand near an old, single, hogan. Several styles of female hogans with red or green tar-paper roofs could be several yards away. The ever present sweat lodge structure would be on the property, too.

ADOBE (AH-DOH-BE)

Mexico City was built on the ruins of a city previously named Tenochtitlán (teh-NOK-teh-TLAN). Before Cortés and the Spaniards destroyed it, the capital city of the Aztecs was the largest city on earth, with a quarter of a million residents. In the countryside, people lived in dark, windowless, one-room earthen homes with hard-packed dirt floors.

In his mural *Great Tenochtitlán* (1929–1945), Mexican artist Diego Rivera depicted the Aztecs' capital city as it was before the Spanish conquest. The city occupied an island in Lake Texcoco. Canals intersected the city and causeways linked it to the mainland.

ADOBE BRICKS

Adobe bricks are made from mud or clay. Soil is mixed with water and a little straw to hold the bricks together. Then the mud and straw mixture is placed in an oblong wooden form until it dries. The forms are removed, and the bricks are left to harden in the sun. Adobe is an important Native American contribution, and adobe buildings are still being built throughout Mexico and the southwestern United States. It is an ideal material for the warm, dry climate because it is a good insulator; it helps keep buildings cool in the summer and warm in the winter.

Most of the buildings were adobe (sun-dried clay) brick with reed mud walls and roofs of reed and grass.

THE LONGHOUSE

The eastern woodlands was the home of three language groups, the Algonquian, Iroquoian, and Siouan. Woodlands houses were of various sizes and shapes, depending on each tribe's social and religious practices. Along the St. Lawrence River, in present-day upper New York State, and west to the shores of Lake Ontario, the most common dwelling of the Iroquois was the longhouse. Framed by bent saplings covered with sheets of bark, it was often more than 100 feet (30 meters) long. Several families lived in the same house, which was often placed inside a high stockade.

THE WIGWAM

The Algonquians to the east, south, and west of Iroquois country constructed many different styles of bark-and-mat-covered structures called wigwams. The Siouans built both woodland and plains-style tipis. Sometimes they constructed earth lodges, depending on the location and the season. The domed wigwam can still be seen today in Indian communities because it is often used as a sweat lodge.

THE PLANK HOUSE AND TOTEM POLE

The fishing and hunting Haida of the Northwest lived on the coast of British Columbia. They built large (sometimes as long as 50 feet [15 meters]) unpainted houses and public buildings out of wide planks and timbers that were pegged together. There was usually an interior pit, too, lined with planks. Several families lived in each house and shared a central hearth. Yet at night they slept in private spaces. Haida houses are famous for their magnificent totem poles near the doorways on which the families' stories and symbols were carved and then brightly colored.

IGLOOS AND OTHER INUIT STRUCTURES

Farther north, during the Alaskan winter, temperatures normally plunged to between 30°F and 50°F below zero (-34°C and -46°C). The natives built their houses to withstand this extreme cold. Thinking of Inuit houses usually brings to mind the igloo, made of blocks of frozen snow. These dome-shaped igloos were built by piling the snow blocks in a spiral. Yet the most common winter structures Inuits built were not igloos. They were structures that used the same heat-saving principle of the snow house but were framed with whalebone, stone, or driftwood. Inuits insulated this structure with layers of dirt, sod, skins, or packed snow.

When summer came, many Inuits moved into some type of tent. It was usually a pole frame covered with sewn caribou, walrus, or seal skins, and it was constructed in many styles. Inuits also built various special-use buildings, such as birth shelters, where the women had their babies.

◇ CLIFF DWELLINGS AND PUEBLOS (PWEB-LOHS) ◇

In sections of Arizona and Colorado dramatic structures can still be seen jutting out from the vertical cliff walls. These were the housing complexes of the cliff dwellers.

Two of the most famous of these apartmentlike clusters still in existence are Montezuma Castle in central Arizona and Mesa Verde in southwestern Colorado. (Montezuma Castle has no connection with Montezuma the emperor of the Aztecs. The castle was built by the Anasazi, at least two hundred years before Montezuma lived.) Although these famous clusters had names like "castle" and "palace," they were not the homes of the aristocracy. The names were given to the ruins by the European explorers and settlers. They assumed that a home so grand must have belonged to someone important such as a king or pope. The truth is that these homes were built by the common people for themselves and their families.

At Mesa Verde, the remains of these cliff dwellings are spectacular. As Jack Weatherford says in *Native Roots*, "Mesa Verde looks almost like a city suspended in midair, hovering above the earth."

At Mesa Verde, Cliff Palace is the largest of the many dwellings that were built on the cliff. It contains buildings up to three stories high with 217 rooms and 23 large circular meeting rooms or religious chambers called kivas.

The builders began with natural ledges and slowly placed one rock on top of another, to stack the buildings. The dwellings were terraced so the roof of each home served as a patio for the story above. The cliff dwellers had excellent protection from their enemies. Yet there were drawbacks to living on steep cliffs. Probably the worst one was having to carry water, supplies, and even dirt up to their homes. They also had to climb down the cliff every day to tend their gardens, which were some distance away on level ground.

There were no staircases. To enter their homes, Indians would climb a ladder to the lower rooftops and go down into the rooms below through the openings. Smaller ladders led to the upper rooms. When not in use, the ladders were pulled up like drawbridges and stored on the roofs.

These clusters of small, multistoried rooms were called pueblos by the Spaniards. For more than a thousand years, the natives belonging to many different language groups who occupied these housing complexes have been known as "Pueblo Indians." Some examples are the Taos, Zuni, Bonito, and Acoma Pueblos.

◇ SOCIAL LIFE ◇

Native Americans' architecture was atuned to their social life. Social rules usually governed where a bride and groom lived after marrying, who helped build their home, where they slept, and the size of their space. Sometimes, group house building was done to show friendship among tribes or between clans.

◇ COMING OF THE EUROPEANS ◇

Indian architecture had been changing for thousands of years, but after the Europeans arrived, the changes became more frequent. New materials such as metal tools and nails became available for Indians. Later, paint and cloth were introduced and finally, milled lumber and molded bricks. In addition, missionaries and U.S. government agents discouraged the Indians from building their traditional houses and continuing their old forms of social life, which they said was causing disease. The truth is, however, that the Europeans caused much of the Indians' disease.

Most Native Americans didn't want to give up their way of life or their traditional architecture. In fact, when a building wasn't used anymore, instead of tearing it down, they kept it, much as we keep landmark buildings today that reflect our history.

◇ NEWCOMERS ADOPT INDIAN ARCHITECTURE AND ◇ CONSTRUCTION FOR HOMES

In New Mexico, very early Spanish settlers adopted Indian architecture, material, and construction methods for their homes. Although their churches were large and European-looking, they were built of mud and brick like the Indian buildings in the community. Most of the buildings in Santa Fe, their capital, were built in the same way the people of the peublos built their homes except for a few changes such as adding Spanish tiles and dividing the buildings into rooms.

As for the colonists, they also borrowed Indian building techniques throughout North America. On the Great Plains, early settlers built their sod houses partially underground, imitating the Indian earth lodges. Being well insulated, these houses stood up well to the extremely cold or hot weather and gave protection during bitter storms. As time went on, however, the colonists were able to afford to have lumber shipped from the woodlands, and their sod homes were abandoned for the traditional European-style, aboveground wooden homes.

On the northern Pacific coast, Europeans easily adopted the plank house because it looked very much like the homes they were used to. They built their rectangular homes above ground with lumber, usually redwood or cedar.

Along the Virginia coast, the newcomers saw that the Algonquian-speaking Indians surrounded their villages with posts buried in the ground and sharpened at the top to give them protection against their enemies. Thinking it a good idea, Europeans used the same type of post. Their structures eventually evolved into the stockade and later, the wooden fort.

◇ INDIAN ARCHITECURE AND AMERICA TODAY ◇

Although the Spaniards and early colonists adopted some Indian building practices, not many of those practices have survived to modern times. The North American Indians mastered the art of making concrete and using lime mortar, and they developed plaster and stucco. Yet none of these technologies have had an impact on high-rise apartments or office buildings built in America today. Some modern buildings may resemble Indian style, but the architect didn't use Indian principles of architecture or science. Jack Weatherford writes in *Indian Givers*, "Unlike native American agriculture, medicine, and political ideas, Indian architecture never influenced Europeans, and it failed to survive on a very large scale even in America."

The architecture of present-day Santa Fe reflects its rich Native American heritage.

One reason that Old World builders did not adopt Indian architecture could have been because they preferred to use arched entryways, windows, and doorways in their churches and public buildings. A church was often topped with a dome, which was also a hemisphere of arches (a half of a sphere bounded by a great circle).

Indian architecture was more like that of ancient China, Greece, and Egypt, where builders used mostly strong angles, straight lines, and parallels in public buildings. But they did use arches in their homes, such as in the early longhouses. Because these buildings consisted of one long room with an arched ceiling, they often resembled European churches. Other Indian structures such as the igloo, kiva, sweat lodge, and hogan all used some form of the arch or the circle as the main feature of their construction.

Early Spanish settlers destroyed or changed most of the Native American architecture. When Cortés ordered Tenochtitlán pulled down, he used parts of buildings and pyramids to fill in the canals. Then he built the streets and churches of Mexico City on the leveled ground. Most of the monumental sites of America were torn down in the same way, and only a few, such as the Anasazi cliff dwellings, have survived.

European colonists coming to America also built on top of Indian sites, but they did not follow the patterns of Indian cities. Therefore, generations of Americans forgot that their towns and cities had been founded by Indians. New World settlers told of carving their homes out of virgin American forests. Even George Washington was said to have ridden his horse through the forest and selected the land beside the Potomac River as the place to build a new capital. The truth is that the city of Washington, D.C., was built on top of Naconchtanke, a former trading town that was home to the Conoy Indians.

In the twentieth century, Native American architecture once again gained some popularity both for its functional form and for its practical building techniques. Prominent architect Frank Lloyd Wright tried to create a new American architecture that blended with nature. He did so by returning to some basic Indian principles that used free-flowing space and warm earth tones. Wright's homes with their new engineering concepts still had some resemblance to the pueblos of Arizona and New Mexico.

Recently, Daniel J. Lenihan and James E. Bradford coauthored an article in *Natural History* magazine mentioning that some basic ancient building principles have been rediscovered in the Southwest. "The homes of the newcomers . . . most are fairly obvious extensions of Native American strategies."

Because a new life was built on an old culture, much of Indian architecture has been lost or buried. Yet some of it still shows through in the buildings of today.

FOUR

Math and Astronomy

Believing that supernatural forces controlled the universe, as did most ancient peoples, including the Christians, the Indians built and aligned their homes and structures with the heavenly bodies. Using nothing more than a pair of crossed sticks or perhaps a couple of buildings lined up as observation points, Indian astronomers studied the movements of the sun, moon, stars, and the planet Venus. From these observations, they developed skills in mathematics, astronomy, and calendar making.

◇ HIEROGLYPHICS ◇

The North American Indians had many languages, but most had no system of writing. To find out what they knew about astronomy, scientists today study their ruins and petroglyphs (rock pictures).

A number of peoples—including the Aztecs, Zapotec, Mixtec, and Maya, who occupied the region extending from central Mexico to Honduras and El Salvador (Mesoamerica)—had a system of writing called hieroglyphics (picture symbols representing words or sounds). These peoples left us written records of their incredible skills in mathematics, astronomy, and calendar making. How long it took the priest-rulers to work out this system of writing and calendars, we don't know. But from the wall panels, monuments, and codices (painted books made from strips of deerskin or pressed tree

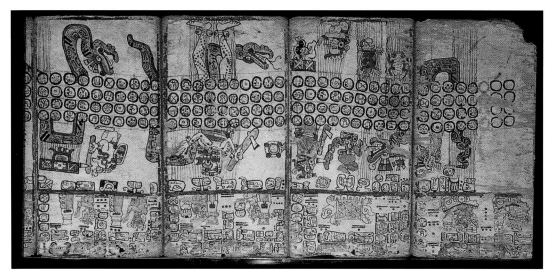

The Madrid Codex, painted on bark paper, records dates appropriate
for various Mayan ceremonies and consists of rows of day glyphs (symbols)
over representations of gods and rain-giving sky serpents.

bark) that were left, modern scientists were able to decipher some of the hieroglyphics. Besides being official records, the codices (singular: codex) contained various notes on astronomy and religious ceremonies, maps, and the corn-planting calendar.

When the Spaniards came to the New World, they considered the codices to be the work of the devil and burned as many as they could find. Unfortunately, much of the wisdom and knowledge of two thousand years or more was destroyed. Only a few codices survived and are now in European museums. However, more and more is being learned each day through excavations in Mexico.

◇ SOLSTICES AND EQUINOXES ◇

The early astronomers were the great explorers of their day. As they watched the heavens, they observed that the sun and stars rose in the east and slowly swept across the sky to sink below the western horizon. Remember, Earth as part of the solar system rotates daily on its axis, and each year it makes a complete revolution from west to east around the sun. After careful study, the early astronomers realized that in the Northern Hemisphere the sun rises and sets farther north in the summer than it does in the winter. That happens because the Northern Hemisphere is slanted toward the sun in the summer and away from the sun in the winter.

The day that the sun rises farthest to the north in the Northern Hemisphere is the summer solstice. It occurs on or about June 21, the longest day of the year, and the first day of summer. Exactly the opposite happens in the Southern Hemisphere on June 21. The southern part of the earth is slanted away from the sun, and it is the day with the least number of daylight hours, the beginning of winter.

The winter solstice occurs on the day of the most southerly sunrise, December 21, the beginning of winter in the north and summer in the south. The two days on which the sun rises halfway between the winter and summer solstices are the spring equinox, March 21, and the autumn equinox, September 21.

The Aztecs and Mayans had many ways to watch and record when the solstices and equinoxes occurred. These events were important so they could devise an accurate calendar to fix the proper days for religious celebrations. Farmers also needed a calendar so they would know when to do their planting and harvesting, when the rainy season would begin, and when the first frost would occur.

◇ MEDICINE WHEELS ◇

One way Native Americans would sky watch was with a device called a Medicine Wheel. It was a huge circle of stone with spokes of stone spreading out from the center. Some of the wheels had boulders piled in the middle, called cairns. Medicine Wheels got their name from the European settlers who thought they looked like wagon wheels and had some magical purpose. Of about fifty wheels that still remain, the most famous is the Bighorn Medicine Wheel in Wyoming.

Two cairns of Wyoming's Bighorn Medicine Wheel seem to align with the rising sun on the summer solstice.

Bighorn Medicine Wheel

The Bighorn Medicine Wheel, in Wyoming, dating from about 1400, is made of limestone slabs and boulders. It was built by the Crow at their summer campgrounds in the Bighorn Mountains. From high on the mountaintop (elevation 10,500 feet [3,200 meters]), they were probably able to track the movements of the sun and stars and to determine the summer solstice. The Medicine Wheel is between 92 and 98 feet (28 and 30 meters) across, and the cairn in the center is 12 feet (3.6 meters) in diameter and 2 feet (.6 meters) high. There are twenty-eight spokes that point to solar and stellar (star) alignments, and six U-shaped cairns around the rim: five outside the circle and one inside. The winter solstice was not observed there though because the Crow left their camp before the weather turned cold.

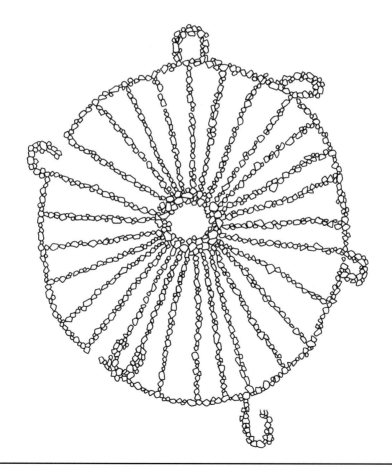

◇ BUILDINGS AND STRUCTURES ◇

Besides Medicine Wheels, Indians had several other methods of observing the skies. Among them was the use of landmarks, such as tall stone columns lined up to cast a shadow at sunset at the equinoxes. Buildings were also used to determine the solstices and equinoxes. One example is Casa Grande, built by the Hohokom around the year 1300, between what is now Phoenix and Tucson, Arizona. Because of its 5-foot (1.5-meter)-thick adobe walls and the maze of rooms, it is thought that this castlelike structure may have doubled as a temple and the home of tribal chiefs. After studying the ruins, scientists found that more than half the window slots in the upper rooms were aligned with the risings and settings of the sun at the solstices and equinoxes. From these window slots, the Hohokom could see the horizon.

The Hohokam astronomical observatory at Casa Grande

Sometimes, a grouping of structures was designed for observing the heavens, such as the temples built at Tenochtitlán (now Mexico City) by the Aztecs. The main temple loomed in the air on a huge pyramid foundation that formed a base for two smaller temples. Astronomers would go across the plaza to the Temple of Quetzalcoatl, and from its tower, at the equinoxes, they could see the sun rise between the two opposite temples.

◇ OBSERVATIONS OF VENUS ◇

Venus had special religious importance to the Maya and Aztecs. About the same size as Earth, Venus is both a morning and an evening star. The astronomers associated it with the god Kulkulcán-Quetzalcoatl, who they believed disappeared into the west with the promise to return sometime out of the eastern sea. Venus seemed to fulfill the prophecy as it disappeared in the west and reappeared as the morning star in the east, like the god in the myth, eight days later.

Mayan astronomers also noted that there were times when Venus rose just before the sun, appeared as a flash of light, and disappeared. This event is called the heliacal rising. After patient study of the planet, the Maya recorded that the heliacal rising occurred every 584 days—a Venus year. That was fairly accurate. Its actual known span is 583.92 days.

Figuring out tables that compared the Venus year with the Earth year (365 days), the Mayan astronomers found that eight Earth years (8 x 365 = 2,920) are equal to five Venus years (5 x 584 = 2,920).

Commenting on these observations, Phyllis Pitluga, senior astronomer at the Adler Planetarium in Chicago, Illinois, said, "One of the most amazing cycles that the Maya and Aztecs were able to observe was the cycle of Venus. They even included the fact that Venus would return to the same place in the sky after 104 years (2 x 52)."

◇ TRACKING THE MOON ◇

Most tribes of North America measured time from one appearance of the crescent of the new moon to the next. They used the moon to measure distance as well. A place could be described as being "two moons away," meaning that it would take two lunar (moon) months on foot to get there. The Aztecs figured the lunar month to be 29.52592 days, which is within seven minutes of our modern measurement. Another extraordinary feat for ancient times was that by keeping careful records of eclipses (when the shadow of one heavenly body is on another), the Maya could predict fairly accurately when the eclipses would occur.

At Chichen Itza, Mexico, the Maya built a round structure called *El Caracol* (the snail). It was dedicated to the great Plumed Serpent god, Kulkulcán-Quetzalcoatl, and designed to be an astronomical laboratory. Astronomers could not only observe the sunrises and sunsets at the solstices and the equinoxes, but also could watch the zenith crossings of the sun. Zenith crossings happen twice a year at noon, when the sun is directly overhead and casts no shadows.

◇ MATHEMATICS ◇

The Aztecs and Maya developed an advanced counting system based on twenty, in contrast with our system of tens (decimal system). Their most remarkable achievement, though, was arriving at the idea of the zero, which no other civilization except the Babylonians and the Hindus had discovered. It was not known in Europe for almost one thousand years. The Maya symbol for "nothing" was usually a shell, a hand, or sometimes a glyph (a symbol that stands for a word, idea, sound, or syllable) of a human head. In the decimal system, we write our numbers horizontally, while the Maya wrote in vertical columns with the lowest values at the bottom and the highest at the top.

◇ WAYS OF MEASURING TIME ◇

Native Americans marked the passing of time mostly so they could plan their annual festivals and seasonal celebrations. At first, time was measured by natural events. Some tribes relied solely on the changes of season and amount of crop growth to guide them. Others fixed their system of festivals on the habits of animals and birds and the changes of the moon. Most tribes figured there were twelve moons to the year, while some considered thirteen to be the correct number. The Kiowa of the plains set a year as twelve-and-a-half moons and carried over the other half to the following year. The Zuni of New Mexico thought of the year as a "passage of time," and the seasons as "steps of the year."

◇ CALENDARS ◇

As Mesoamericans used their knowledge of astronomy to determine the length of the year and the changes of the seasons, they recorded these observations on calendars. They measured time by the most accurate calendars in the ancient world. To them, time was controlled by gods, good and bad. Each god was connected to a certain number and was represented by a specific glyph.

The Maya guided their lives by three interrelated calendars, inherited from other Mesoamericans: One was religious (Tzolkin); the second, solar (Haab), and the third, the Calendar Round. We know the Maya measured days, but there is no evidence that they measured hours or minutes. The Tzolkin, or book of the days, was sacred. Each day's name had a number, one through thirteen, combined with one of the twenty day names, such as Ahau and Akbal, which worked out to 260 possible combinations.

The same system of counting was used by all Mesoamericans, but the day names varied from group to group. The Aztecs had day names such as Ozomatli (monkey) or Xochitl (flower) with the numbers one through thirteen. The calendar begins with One Alligator and the next name is Two Wind, and so on. After 260 days from the beginning of the count, One Alligator comes up again. Each number-name combination had its own special fortune, good or bad. Thirteen, considered an unlucky number today, was thought to be a good and sacred number.

The priests were the only ones who knew how to use the calendar to predict when the good gods would make good things happen and when evil gods might cause things to go wrong. They were the ones who picked the best day for an event such as a wedding or a religious festival.

Among the Zapotec, Mixtec, and Aztecs, children were often named for the day of their birth. For example, a boy might be named Six Ozomatli. To give the day name, a hieroglyphic sign was used; a dot was used for the number one, and a bar for the number five. Thus if Six Ozomatli were to write his name it would look like this:

The solar calendar, or Haab, was used for everyday affairs. It measured the time between one crossing of the zenith by the sun and the next crossing. This measurement the Maya figured as exactly 365.242500 days, and it is almost the same as our modern measurement of 365.241298 days. But the Mayan calendar was divided into eighteen months, where ours is twelve. The Maya and Aztecs also divided each month into four weeks of five days, with a leap year similar to ours. The five days that remained were added at the end of the year and were believed to be dangerous and unlucky. Anyone born on these days would have an ill-fated future. People fasted and obeyed sacred rules to avoid evil happenings.

Combining the 365-day Haab calendar with the 260-day Tzolkin like two interlocking cogwheels produced the Calendar Round, a fifty-two-year cycle of 18,980 days. The Aztecs thought of time as running in cycles. At the end of a fifty-two-year cycle, special rituals and festivals were held to "tie up the years." Reeds representing the years were actually tied into bundles and a new cycle began. The Hopi devised a lunisolar calendar with thirteen lunar months, based on where the sun sets on the western horizon. This calendar was adjusted so that it was never more than a day off for calculating their solar festival. Some modern Hopi still use the solar calendar.

Our calendars today are also based on the cycles of the sun. But most of the calculations were arrived at independently from the Indian calendars.

FIVE

Tools, Weapons, and Technology

Ancient peoples had to provide for their families the same as people do today. Wherever they lived, they needed food, some type of shelter, clothing, and utensils. To supply these things, weapons and tools had to be devised. The knives and scrapers (to scrape hides) that archaeologists have found are proof that early peoples killed and skinned wild animals, ate their flesh, and used their pelts for clothing. In fact, they used every part of the animal they killed, leaving no waste. The digging sticks and hoes left behind tell us how they farmed.

As for weapons of war, the Indians were no match for the European guns or steel swords and lances. While the natives fought with arrows and spears tipped with stone and used atlatls (spear throwers), the Europeans, who got gunpowder from the Chinese, learned to cast metal cannons, which they mounted on wheels that were pulled by animals.

◇ BONE TOOLS ◇

Stacey Pyne, education curator at the Lake County Museum in Illinois, said, "Remember, there was no corner hardware store. Indians had to make tools and weapons out of whatever they found in the world around them, mostly bone, stone, wood and sometimes shell."

Bone tools were the easiest to make. Many Indians would chip animal bones into sharp slivers, and the slivers became awls, knives, and scrapers. They used antlers for picks and animal shoulder blades for hoes.

◇ STONE TOOLS ◇

Some Native Americans made it a practice to look for the right kinds of stones to make into tools. Stone toolmaking took time and patience. First, the stone had to be hacked into shape with another stone. Then, it was chipped to make a sharp edge. If a smooth edge was needed, sand and water helped grind out the roughness.

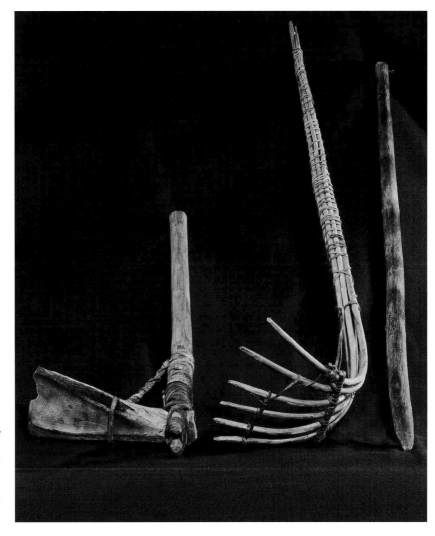

Early farm tools of the Hidatsa and Mandan Indians of the Northwest: a bone hoe, a wooden rake and digging stick

◇ HAMMERS AND AXES ◇

To make tools such as hammers and axes, a strong stone such as granite was used—one that wouldn't split when it was pounded. Every tribe had a hammer even if it was just a chunk of stone, but axes were not as plentiful.

Instead of axes, the Northwestern tribes, such as the Salish, Tlingit, and Kwakiutl, who did much woodworking, made adzes. Adzes were similar to axes but had a curved blade and were made of minerals such as hard serpentine or jade.

◇ ARROWHEADS AND SCRAPERS ◇

To make arrowheads and scrapers, a different kind of stone was needed, one that would split similarly to the way ice is split by chopping it with an ice pick. Almost any variety of fine-grained or glasslike stone was used, such as flint, chert, or the black volcanic glass obsidian.

These stones were good for all cutting tools. To make a tool, the worker placed the edge of his stone on a piece of wood, set a bone chisel against it, and hammered until a chip flew off. After knocking off several chips in a row, he had a cutting edge somewhat like the jagged edge of a modern bread knife. Longer stones became knives, shorter stones were used as scrapers, spearheads, and arrowheads.

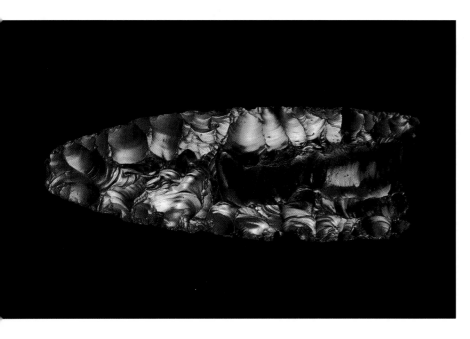

Obsidian, said to be sharper than surgical steel, was used by some cultures for surgical procedures. This obsidian Clovis point was unearthed at Blackwater Draw, New Mexico.

SANDIA, CLOVIS, AND FOLSOM DISCOVERIES

The people who lived in Sandia Cave, New Mexico, possibly as long as twenty thousand years ago, left heavy, sharp spear points that were up to 4 inches (10 centimeters) long and bayonet-shaped.

Several thousand years after the Sandia people, another group called the Clovis people (so named because they hunted mammoths near Clovis, New Mexico) left well-crafted ivory and stone spearheads of about the same size as the Sandia spearheads. They were bullet-shaped though and grooved or "fluted" partway up the face. Clovis points were first discovered in New Mexico in the 1930s, and later, thousands of similar fluted points were found in nearly every part of North America.

About ten thousand years ago, the famous Folsom point came into use. It is famous because it provided the first proof of the existence of the American Glacial Man. In 1927, near Folsom, New Mexico, a Folsom point was found imbedded between the ribs of an Ice Age buffalo. It was beautifully crafted, light, smaller than either the Clovis or Sandia, and distinguished by a long groove or "fluting" running up each face.

Pueblo women often ground corn in groups of three, each using a stone of different fineness. The bottom stone was a flat slab called a metate. The grinding was done by rubbing the grains across it with another stone, called the mano (held in hands). The Illinois used a mortar (vessel) and a club-shaped hand tool called a pestle to pound, grind, or mash grain.

The metate and mano have been used for centuries to grind corn for flour.

After a while people discovered that tools were easier to use if they had handles. The stone tool was usually grooved or cut and fitted inside a forked stick. Some Indians bound the tool to the handle with twisted plant fiber or a piece of leather. But the material considered to be the best for binding tools, if available, was animal sinew (a tendon). The sinew was put on wet and wound tightly. As it dried, the sinew would shrink and become as hard as twine.

Recently, a team of scientists lead by the Smithsonian Institution's archaeologist Dennis Stanford used flaked stone tools to cut up a dead elephant in an attempt to learn more about how hunting peoples may have butchered fallen mammoths twelve thousand years ago. They hacked, sawed, and chopped with replica tools of obsidian (natural glass) hafted onto wooden handles. They said the work was very hard, but they were able to do it.

Native peoples also had wooden tools, such as the long, wooden digging stick used for planting and cultivating, on which the stump of one branch had been left a few inches from the bottom. In this way the farmer's foot could help with the digging. For weeding, the worker, in a kneeling position, used a wooden hoe shaped like a sword and sharpened along one edge. As it was pulled along the ground, the hoe cut off the tops of the weeds.

◇ SPEARS AND ATLATLS (AT-LAT-ELS) ◇

Long ago, hunters made spears carved from mammoth leg bones that were straightened by boiling them in water until soft. Later, hunters threw wooden spears at animals in order to fell them. After a while they added stone tips to the spears. These tips, called points, were made of a hard stone such as flint. Many of these points of various sizes and shapes have been found at digs.

Thousands of years before the bow and arrow appeared in the Americas, people carried spear throwers, or atlatls. The atlatl, an awesome tool, was a grooved wooden device, a sort of launch-pad handle that gave the hunter an ad-

The atlatl consisted of a grooved, wooden bar up to 3 feet (1 meter) long from which a spear could be launched.

vantage by adding to the length of his arm. It also made it possible to throw the spear straighter, so the spear tip hit its target with greater force.

◇ TRAPS AND NETS ◇

Wooden pens were used as traps into which game was driven. Many Indians made spring traps and deadfalls that dropped a weight on the animal or caught its foot in a noose. The Nootka in the Pacific Northwest constructed traps with heavy logs into which they drove deer and then harpooned them. The harpoon was like a spear with a rope attached. It was thrown by hand or with an atlatl. The hunter kept hold of the rope so that the speared animal could not get away.

Nets of all sizes were made out of twisted cord from the inner bark of trees or from plant fiber. The nets were used to catch fish or, on land, to snare ducks and rabbits. Some Native Americans fished with hooks made of bone or sharpened wood; other fishermen used spears. The atlatl and spear were also used for fishing by the Alaska natives and Pacific Coast tribes. It was eventually replaced by the bow and arrow, which became the main weapon not only in hunting, but also in warfare.

◇ BOWS AND ARROWS ◇

Bows were made in various shapes, depending on the wood available. The bowstring was usually made of twisted plant fiber. Those who hunted on foot often used bows 6 feet (1.8 meters) long and with very little curve. Shorter bows had more curve, and the string was made of deer sinew; the shorter the bow, the stronger it had to be. Horsemen used these short bows.

Arrows were usually about 3 feet (1 meter) long. They were made of a light, straight wood or sometimes of reed. To control flight, two or three feathers were often used on each arrow at the end of the shaft near the nock (a notch or groove at the end of the arrow where the bowstring fits). Each tribe had its own way of putting on the feathers. The arrow used by the Northwest Indians had a long shaft and a short feather. The arrows of the Plains Indians were just the opposite, having a short shaft and a long feather.

For small game, the tip of the arrow was made of sharpened wood. If it was meant to kill deer or men, the tip was made of stone. A man usually put his personal mark on his arrow so he could find it and use it again.

The bow and arrow had important advantages over the spear and atlatl. The atlatl

HARNESSING THE WIND

Navajo Indian Steve Grey is a mechanical engineer and the head of the Lawrence Livermore National Laboratory's American Indian Program in Shiprock, New Mexico. He is committed to a project to bring electricity to more homes in the Navajo reservation through the use of wind power rather than through the more environmentally harmful use of coal. Important to Grey is that the Navajos have a strong voice in the engineering decisions of the windmill farm and that any excess power produced would be sold to other utilities to bring in needed income.

A rubber tapper today near the town of Xapuri, Brazil. After collecting the sap from the rubber trees, he brings the collected rubber back home, pours it into a basin, and then cooks it over an open fire to thicken it. Here he is pouring the rubber over a stick. He will then place the stick over smoke in order to congeal and harden it. Next, the rubber is removed from the stick and rolled flat to be pressed into bales.

could be thrown farther than the handheld spear but the hunter had to stand up and take a step or two in order to throw. Then he had to fit another spear of at least 6 feet (1.8 meters) to the atlatl and throw again. It took so much time that the enemy or quarry could disappear. In contrast, an archer armed with a short bow could shoot from a hiding place behind a bush or boulder. He could then fit another short arrow from the bunch held in his other hand or in a quiver and fire again without giving away his position. The bow and spear thrower gave about the same amount of speed to a stone-tipped missile, but the bow could be fired faster and more accurately.

◇ TOMAHAWKS ◇

For fighting, sometimes a heavy, wooden clublike weapon with a knot at one end was used. Some eastern tribes set a sharp stone point in the knot. This weapon became the famous tomahawk. Fur traders copied the weapon and added a steel point. Finally, it developed into a small axe.

◇ RUBBER ◇

When discussing Indian technology, we must mention rubber. Because of rubber, there have been many technological innovations. Early Indians along the Amazon River of Brazil extracted the milky juice, or latex, from the tall rubber tree they called cahuchi (*Hevea brasiliensis*) and cured it over a fire. They used the rubber to make items such as balls for their children, raincoats, rubber-soled shoes, rubber bottles, and ropes. Europeans knew about rubber but paid no attention to it. They were more interested in gold, silver, and tobacco that could make them rich. It wasn't until about three hundred years after Columbus that Europeans realized rubber was a useful product.

When the Indians heated the rubber, they mixed it with sulfur to make it stronger and remove its stickiness and bad odor. This process is called vulcanization. It was not until 1839, when an American inventor, Charles Goodyear, stumbled onto a laboratory method of vulcanization, that the process became known to white society. The "discovery" led the way to many new inventions and helped in the development of the automobile.

Thomas Macintosh, an Englishman, used rubber to fashion a type of raincoat that is still worn today. Many shoe manufacturers began using rubber to make their shoes waterproof. In homes, schools, and offices more and more products, such as rubber bands, erasers, and doormats, were made of rubber.

Electricity had been known for a century, but until scientists insulated metal wires with rubber, people didn't know how to make electricity work for them. Rubber insulation opened the era of electrification.

Because we have so many uses for rubber today, chemists have been trying to make a synthetic product that is exactly like rubber. Botanists are also looking for other shrubs or plants that are drought resistant and will produce a good latex yield.

CONCLUSION

What does a new look at the science and technology of the early American Indian tell us? For one, we find that Indians were the first ecologists. Early native peoples had a deep religious respect for the earth and all it holds, as do Indians today. Because they revere nature, Indians believe that humans must live in harmony with all the natural elements. Although humans have their place in the universe, according to Indian science, or "indigenous" science as it is sometimes called, that place is no better or worse than that of the animals, birds, trees, soil, sun, or moon.

Many legends and myths were spread about Indians by the European invaders, but their true story was not really known. Although there were some individuals and groups on both sides that tried to create trust and understanding between the cultures, they were never strong or powerful enough to overcome the mutual misunderstandings. We are just beginning to realize that the Indian peoples had a rich, spiritual life, a diversified culture, and a body of wisdom that we know little about.

How did early Indian peoples rank with those of the Old World? Non-Indians had a certain Eurocentric way of viewing the Indian civilizations that they have passed on to their descendants. It was the view that Euro-American values, religions, and achievements were much more advanced than the Indians' values. To them, Indians were inferior peoples who had barbaric customs and were even dangerous to "civilized" people.

In truth, New World cultures had superior know-how in farming and technology, and they were ahead of the Old World in their knowledge of pharmacology. Indian calendars were far more sophisticated than that of the Europeans, and the Indians of Mexico had a math system superior to the numerical systems then used by the Spaniards.

Poised at the beginning of a new century, we are becoming more aware of the fragility of our ecosystem. Knowledge of the cultures of the early American Indians takes on a greater importance than ever before. Today, our system of Western science is beginning to look to Indian science, with its holistic approach to life, for survival ideas. We should make the changes that will guarantee future generations a good life with pure air and water, fertile land, nutritious food, and spiritual health.

Listen again to the words of Totanka Yotanka (Sitting Bull), "In the morning when I walk barefoot on its soil I can hear the very heart of the holy earth."

FOR MORE INFORMATION

The best source of information about Native Americans is your public library. Libraries have computers, reference books such as encyclopedias, and a great deal of material published by federal agencies. They also have books on the history of Indian tribes and various aspects of Indian life, and magazines with articles about Indians. Librarians are trained to help you find materials or to obtain them from other libraries through an interlibrary loan.

FURTHER READING

Faber, Harold. *The Discoverers of America*. New York: Charles Scribner's Sons, 1992.

Ferio, Jeri. *Native American Doctor: The Story of Susan La Flesche Picotte*. Minneapolis: Carolrhoda Books, 1991.

Green, Rayna. *Women in American Indian Society*. New York: Chelsea House, 1992.

Hoyt-Goldsmith, Diane. *Pueblo Storyteller*. New York: Holiday House, 1991.

Tannenbaum, Beulah, and Tannenbaum, Harold E. *Science of the Early American Indians*. New York: Franklin Watts, 1988.

Wolfson, Evelyn. *From the Earth to Beyond the Sky: Native American Medicine*. New York: Houghton, 1993.

Selected Bibliography

Ballantine, Betty, and Ballantine, Ian, eds. *The Native Americans*. Atlanta: Turner Publishing, 1993.

Brandon, William. *Indians*. New York: American Heritage, 1989. Also, *American Heritage Book of Indians*.

Encyclopedia of Discovery and Exploration. The Conquest of North America. New York: Doubleday, 1973.

Kopper, Philip, et al., eds. *The Smithsonian Book of North American Indians Before the Coming of the Europeans*. Washington, D.C.: Smithsonian Books, 1986.

Mails, Thomas E. *The Mystic Warriors of the Plains*. New York: Mallard Press, 1991 ed.

Navokov, Peter, and Easton, Robert. *Native American Architecture*. New York: Oxford University Press, 1989.

Plotkin, Mark J. *Tales of a Shaman's Apprentice*. New York: Viking Press, 1993.

Stone, Eric, M.D. *Medicine Among the American Indians*. New York: Ams Press, 1978 ed.

Stoutenburgh, John, Jr. *Dictionary of the American Indian*. New York: Bonanza Books, 1990 ed.

Viola, Herman J. *After Columbus: The Smithsonian Chronicle of the North American Indians*. Washington, D.C.: Smithsonian Books, 1990.

Vogel, Virgil J. *American Indian Medicine*. Norman, Okla.: University of Oklahoma Press, 1970.

Warner, John Anson. *The Life and Art of the North American Indian*. Edison, N.J.: Chartwell Books, 1990 ed.

Weatherford, Jack M. *Indian Givers*. New York: Crown, 1988.

———. *Native Roots*. New York: Crown, 1991.

Where to Write

American Indian Science and Engineering Society
5661 Airport Blvd.
Boulder, CO 80301-2339
Website: **http://bioc02.uthscsa.edu/aisesnet.html**

Bureau of Indian Affairs—Ask for pamphlet *American Indians Today*. Also has lists of other publications by Government Printing Office, lists and addresses of Indian organizations and services.

U.S. Department of the Interior
1849 C Street NW
Washington, DC 20240-0001
Website: **http://info.er.usgs.gov/doi/bureau-indian-affairs.html**

Indian Health Service—Has information on Indian health matters.
U.S. Department of Health and Human Services, Parklawn Building
5600 Fishers Lane
Rockville, MD 20857
Website: **http://www.ihs.gov/IHSMAIN. html**

Bureau of the Census—For the latest numbers.
U.S. Department of Commerce,
    Racial Statistics Branch
Population Division
Washington, DC 20233
Website: **http://popindex.princeton.edu/ browse/v55/n2/t.html**

Rodale Institute Research Center—For new seed research.
Rodale Institute
611 Siegfriedale Rd.
Kutztown, PA 19530

Native Seeds/SEARCH—Ancient seeds. Packets can be purchased (free to Native Americans). Also sells books and Tarahumara Indian crafts. Write for catalog.
Native Seeds/SEARCH
2509 N. Campbell Ave. #325
Tucson, AZ 85719
Website: **http://desert.net/seeds/home.htm**

Map Sales—For a large map of Indian reservations (26" x 42"), send $2.75 plus $1.00 postage. File Reference number US5666.
Department of the Interior
U.S. Geological Survey
P.O. Box 25286, Federal Center
Denver, CO 80225

U.S. Fish and Wildlife Service—For youth programs in natural resources and career opportunities for Native American youths.
U.S. Dept. of the Interior
1 Federal Drive
Fort Snelling, MN 55111-4056

Audiovisuals

BreakThrough: The Changing Face of Science in America. Profiles American Indians and other scientists of color. Six hour-long programs. Produced by Blackside, Inc. Available through PBS Video (1-800-328-PBS1).

Native American Public Broadcasting Consortium—Large quantity of video programs available for rent or purchase. Free catalog. Topics: history, culture, education, arts, economic development.
Native American Public Broadcasting Consortium
P.O. Box 8311
Lincoln, NB 68501

Keepers of the Earth: Native American Stories and Environmental Activities for Children (ISBN 1-55591-027-0 cl bk) by Michael J. Caduto and Joseph Bruchac; *Stories from Keepers of the Earth* (094-7) narrated by Joseph Bruchac; *Keepers of the Earth/Native American Stories* (099-8 tape), Golden, CO: Fulcrum Publishing, 1989.

Historical Sites, Monuments, and Museums

Ah-Tha-Thi-Ki Museum—Seminole Museum, a good place to visit and learn. There is a school on the premises, and you can see videos of past and present life of Seminole Indians.
5845 S. State Road 7
Fort Lauderdale, FL 33314

Alaska State Museum—Has many Indian and Eskimo artifacts of the Aleut, Athapaskan, and Indians of the Northwest Coast. See an excellent display of items relating to Indian life in Juneau.
Whittier St.
Juneau, AK 99811
Website: **http://ccl.alaska.edu/local/museum/home.html**

British Columbia Provincial Museum—Excellent exhibits of Indian cultural heritage. There are extraordinary masks, totem poles, carvings, and textiles.
675 Belleville St.
Victoria, BC V8V 1X4

Cahokia Mounds State Historic Site—Archaeological remains of a once flourishing civilization.
P.O. Box 681
Collinsville, IL 62234
Website: **http://www.state.il.us/HPA/CAHOKIAM.HTM**

Canadian Museum of Civilization
100 Laurier Street
P.O. Box 3100, Station B
Hull, Quebec J8X 4H2, Canada
Website: **http://www.cmcc.muse.**

Casa Grande National Monument. You can see ruins of a huge four-story building constructed by Indians six hundred years ago.
P.O. Box 518
Coolidge, AZ 85228
Website: **http://www.nps.gov/cagr/**

Cherokee Historical Association—Museum of the Cherokee Indian. Has a good research library and a large collection of Cherokee artifacts. The Oconaluftee Indian Village is on the grounds. There is a drama about the Cherokee here every summer in the outdoor theater.
U.S. Hwy 441 N.
P.O. Box 770-A
Cherokee, NC 28719

Field Museum of Natural History—Has a major collection of Native American art and artifacts.
Roosevelt Rd. at Lake Shore Dr.
Chicago, IL 60605
Website: **http://www.vol.it/mirror/field/museum**

Mesa Verde National Park. You can see well-preserved ancient cliff dwellings here and other works of early peoples.
Mesa Verde National Park, CO 81330
Website: **http://mesaverde.org/mvnp.html**

Montezuma Castle National Monument—See ruins of a five-story cliff dwelling built by the Sinagua in the twelfth and thirteenth centuries. It is probably one of the best-preserved cliff dwellings in the United States.
P.O. Box 219
Camp Verde, AZ 86322
Website: **http://www.nps.gov/moca/**

National Museum of the American Indian, Smithsonian Institution—Collection of one million objects, spanning more than ten thousand years. About 70 percent of the collection represents cultures in the United States and Canada; 30 percent, cultures of Central and South America. Exhibition and programs.
The George Gustav Heye Center Alexander Hamilton U.S. Custom House
One Bowling Green
New York, NY 10004

The National Museum of the American Indian on the Mall in Washington, D.C., is scheduled to open in 2002.
Website: **http://www.si.edu/nmai**

Seneca-Iroquois National Museum—Changing exhibits here show various aspects of Seneca and Iroquois life. Displays beautiful artifacts and cultural treasures.
P.O. Box 442
Broad Street Extension
Salamanca, NY 14779

Internet Resources

There is a wealth of information on the Internet about Native American cultures. Many sites can be accessed through NativeWeb (**http://www.maxwell.synedu/nativeweb/**). Museums that have websites usually provide links to other resources as well.

G L O S S A R Y

adobe—a mixture of wet clay used for mortar or sun-dried bricks in the Southwest; sometimes reinforced with fiber

artifact—a product of human workmanship; one of the simpler products of primitive art, as distinguished from a natural object

atlatl—a grooved, wooden device used to throw a spear

Aztec—a general term for the civilization of several Indian groups of central Mexico that had similar languages and customs during the two centuries before the Spanish conquest. One of these groups is the Mexica, more commonly known as the Aztecs.

bent frame—a frame of small saplings set into the ground and then bent and tied together to form a dome-shaped structural frame

cairn—a pile of stones at the center of a Medicine Wheel

chinampa (a floating garden)—artificial island made by digging canals and draining a swamp

clan—a group in a tribe whose members believe they share a common ancestor (human or mythical); membership evolves from mother's or father's line; generally members are forbidden to marry within the clan

codices—handwritten, painted books made of deerskin or pressed tree bark where Aztecs and Maya scribes recorded in hieroglyphics their astronomical and mathematical knowledge, agricultural instructions, and crafts

eclipse—when the shadow of one heavenly body is cast on another

equinox—one of two days of the year when the sun crosses the plane of the earth's equator, making night and day of equal length all over the earth

glyph—a carved figure or character in a writing system. A glyph stands for a word, idea, sound, or syllable.

hieroglyphic—a system of writing where pictures represent words or syllables

kiva—special chambers, often underground, that are used for meetings and religious rituals

Kulkulcán—the plumed or feathered serpent, Creator God of the Mayas. See Quetzalcoatl.

longhouse—a general term for a long, multifamily dwelling and identified with Iroquoian buildings; now often used to mean various traditional-style Indian meetinghouses

maize—the grain we call corn

obsidian—a volcanic glass, usually black or very dark colored

petroglyph—a carving on stone or rock

pictograph—a painting on any type of material such as animal skins, tree bark, or shells

pueblo—a communal dwelling; also Indians who lived in a pueblo

Quetzalcoatl—Aztec god worshiped as the inventor and patron of arts and crafts and the author of Mexican civilization. He is identical with the Mayan Kulkulcán.

reed—a tall grass with hollow, jointed stalks

solstice—one of the two days in a year when the sun is at its greatest distance from the celestial equator

Tenochtitlán—the city founded by the Mexica in 1325 within present-day Mexico City

tipi—an American Indian conical tent used by most of the Great Plains tribes

totem pole—a name for cedar poles on the Northwest Coast carved with a series of symbols and erected in front of a dwelling

wigwam—a specific term for the dome-shaped winter dwelling of certain tribes

A C K N O W L E D G M E N T S

The author and editors wish to thank the following for their assistance in the preparation of this book: U.S. Department of the Interior, Bureau of Indian Affairs, Washington, D.C.; Smithsonian Institution, National Museum of Natural History, Washington, D.C., and Office of Anthropology, Washington, D.C.; National Museum of the American Indian, New York, New York Resource Center, Gaetana De Gennaro, Resource Center, Washington, D.C.; Dan Agent, Director of Public Affairs, Cherokee Nation, Tahlequah, Oklahoma; National Academy of Science, Washington, D.C., Noel Vietneyer, senior program officer, and Mark Dafforn, research associate; Native American Rights Fund, John E. Echohawk, executive director; Jerry B. Howard, curator of anthropology, Mesa Southwest Museum, Phoenix, Arizona; American Indian College Fund, New York, New York, Kristen Simone, director of media relations, Holly Falk, assistant director of media relations; Ah-Tha-Thi-Ki Museum—Seminole Tribes of Florida, Tom Gallaher, development director, and William Cypress; Cherokee Historical Association, Cherokee, North Carolina, Alan Smith, operations assistant; Department of the Interior, Fish and Wildlife Service, Minnesota, Barbara A. Milne, assistant regional director of human resources; Adler Planetarium, Chicago, Illinois, Phyllis Pitluga, senior astronomer; Native Seeds/SEARCH, Tucson, Seeds of Change, Santa Fe, and Seed Savers Exchange, Decorah, Iowa; Rodale Institute Research Center, Kutztown, Pennsylvania; Shaman Pharmaeuticals, San Francisco, California, Mary Anne McMullen Heins, corporate communications manager; Lake County Museum, Wauconda, Illinois, Stacey Pyne, education curator; Dept. of Tourism, Pierre, South Dakoka, Jeane Wharton and Ward B. Whitman, AIA, Sioux Falls, South Dakota; Native Visions, Don Perret and Joanne Perret.

For excellent manuscript assistance: Betzy Barnett and Janet Carlson, library aides, and Dan Salway, Harve Gallup, Linda and Michael Dunn, Richard Raphael, Jeanette Allison, LaVerel and Samuel Rashkow.

INDEX

acne, treatment of, 26
adobes, 35–36
adzes, 56
Algonquians, 36, 40
alternative medicine, 22
amaranth, 18, 19
American Indian Medicine, 25
amputation, 29–30
Anasazi, 37, 42
Arapahos, 24
architecture, 32, 40, 42–43
    colonists' use of Indian, 40
    European influence on, 39
    Spanish settlers, adoption
        of Indian, 40
arrowheads, 56
arrows, 60, 63
aspirin, 22
astronomy, 45–50
atlatls, 54, 59–60, 63

awls, 55
axes, 56, 63
Aztecs, 19, 23, 35, 44, 46, 49,
    50, 51, 52

Banting, Frederick, 22
Bighorn Medicine Wheel, 46–
    47
Bird, Kendra, 27
bone tools, 55
bows, 60, 63
bricks, adobe, 36
bronchitis, treatment of, 29

Caddos, 23
Cahokia, Illinois, 33
Calendar Round, 52–53
calendars, 51–53
canals, 15–17
cancer, treatment of, 27

Cardinal, Douglas, 42
Cartier, Jacques, 26–27
Casa Grande, 48
cascara sagrada, 22
catarrh, 29
Catawbas, 29
Cherokees, 28
Cheyennes, 23
children, naming, 52
chinampas, 17
Chippewas. *See* Objibwas
cinchona, 26
cliff dwellings, 37, 39
Clovis points, 56, 57
codices, 44–45
colds, treatment of, 29
Comanches, 23, 29
corn, 11–12, 58
cotton, 15
Creeks, 26

crop diversity, preservation of, 19

Crows, 47

culture, 65

Dafforn, Mark, 18

Dakotas, 29

Delawares, 26

diabetes, 30

diet, 22

dislocations, 28

drums, healing with, 24

earth lodges, 34, 40

Easton, Robert, 32

ecology, 65

equinoxes, 46, 48, 49

Etowah, Georgia, 33

farm tools, 59

floating gardens, 17

Folsom points, 57

Fox. See Mesquakies

fractures, 28

Garfield, James, 28

gastrointestinal disturbances, 28

genetics, 12

Geronimo, 23

Goodyear, Charles, 63

Grey, Steve, 61

Haidas, 36–37

hallucinations, 23

hammers, 56

harpoons, 60

Healing Forest Conservancy, 31

health standards, 25

Hidatsas, 55

hieroglyphics, 44–45, 52

hilling method, 12

hoes, 55

hogans, 34–35, 42

Hohokam, 15–17, 48

hominy, 11–12

Hopi, 53

horsemint, 26

household tools, 58–59

Huichols, 23

Hurons, 27

hybridization, 12

hypnosis, 22

igloos, 37, 42

Illinois, 58

Incas, 18

Indian Givers, 40

insulin, discovery of, 22

Inuits, 37

Iroquois, 12, 36

irrigation, 15–17

jewelweed, 26

jimsonweed plants, 25

juniper leaves as remedy for cold, 29

Kiowas, 23, 51

kivas, 38, 42

knives, 55

Kwakiutl, 56

laboratory, astronomical, 50

Lind, James, 27

lion's heart, 26

longhouses, 36, 42

lung infections, treatment of, 29

Macintosh, Thomas, 63

malaria, 26

Mandans, 55

mano, 58

massage, 22, 28

mathematics, 50

Mayans, 44, 46, 49, 50, 51, 52

medicine bags, 24, 24–25

medicine men, 21, 23, 25–26, 28, 29, 30, 31

Medicine Wheels, 46

Menominees, 25, 29

Mesa Verde, 37, 38

mescaline, 23

Mesquakies, 29

metate, 58

milpas, 12

Mixtecs, 44

Montezuma Castle, 37

moon, tracking the, 49

mortar, 58

mounds, 32–34

Moundville, Alabama, 33, 34

Mt. Pleasant, Jane, 14

Nabokov, Peter, 32

Naconchtanke, 43

National Academy of Science, 18

Native American Architecture, 32

Native Roots, 37

Native Seeds/SEARCH, 19, 30

Navajos, 14, 34–35, 61

nets, 60
Nootkas, 60

Ojibwas, 29
Omahas, 29
Onondagas, 25
Osages, 24

Paiute, 17
Pawnees, 29, 34
Pemaquid, 12
pennyroyal as remedy for cold, 29
pestle, 58
petroglyphs, 44
petroleum jelly, 22
peyote, 23–24
Pharmacopoeia of the United States of America, 22
picks, 55
plank houses, 36–37, 40
planting, 12
poison ivy, 26
Poncas, 29
potatoes, 14–15
Potawatomis, 24
Pueblo Indians, 17, 39, 58
pueblos, 39

quinine, 26
quinoa, 18, 19

rattles, healing with, 24
red cedar as remedy for cold, 29

religious calendars, 51
respiratory diseases, treatment of, 29
Rivera, Diego, 35
Rodale Research Center, 18
rubber, 62–64

Salish, 56
Sandia points, 57
scrapers, 54, 55, 56
scurvy, 26–27
Shaman Pharmaceuticals, 30–31
shamans, 23
Shoshone, 28
Siouans, 36
Sioux, 24, 28
Sitting Bull, 23, 66
Snake Dance, 26
snakebites, 25–26
social life, architecture and, 39
solar calendars, 52
solstices, 46, 48
spears, 59–60, 60, 63
Spiro, Oklahoma, 33
stone tools, 55
stress management, 22
surgery, 29–30
survival, holistic approach to, 66
sweat lodges, 28, 35, 36, 42

Tales of a Shaman's Apprentice, 30
taxol, 27

Temple of Quetzalcoatl, 49
Tenochtitlán, 35, 42, 49
"three sisters," 12, 13, 14
time, methods of measuring, 51–53
Tlingit, 56
tobacco, 15
tomahawks, 63
Tohono O'odham, 30
Totanka Yotanka (Sitting Bull), 9, 23, 66
totem poles, 37
Traditional Native American Farmers Association, 19
traps, 60
Tucson Botanical Gardens, 19

Utes, 29

values, 65
Venus, observations of, 49
visualization, 22
vitamin C, 27
Vogel, Virgil J., 25
vulcanization, 63

Wampanoag, 12
Weatherford, Jack, 37, 40
wigwams, 36
wounds, 28
Wright, Frank Lloyd, 43

Zapotecs, 44
Zuni, 51

Fern G. Brown is the author of over thirty books for children, both fiction and nonfiction. She holds a master's degree in education from Northwestern University and has taught in the Chicago public school system. She is often called on to give talks to schoolchildren. Her book *Behind the Scenes at the Horse Hospital* won the Chicago Public Library's Carl Sandburg award. Her latest book is *Daisy and the Girl Scouts: The Story of Juliette Low*. Ms. Brown lives in Riverwoods, Illinois.